The Official
Kid Pix™ Activity Book

By Steve and
Ruth Bennett

RANDOM HOUSE
ELECTRONIC PUBLISHING

New York

Manufactured in the United States of America

First Edition

ISBN: 0-679-74685-4

0 9 8 7 6 5 4 3 2

New York, Toronto, London, Sydney, Auckland

Acknowledgements

Numerous people helped turn the idea for this book into a reality. First and foremost, we'd like to thank Michael Mellin, our publisher, for encouraging us to write the book and for supporting the project throughout. Our eagle-eyed editor, Tracy Smith, worked with us as a "partner-in-crime," helping us to shape ideas and make sure we provided enough information so that people could duplicate our ideas. Mia McCroskey, our production editor, offered great design ideas and shepherded the project from disk to book.

We'd also like to thank our Broderbund contacts, Susan Lee Merrow, Marianne Mullins, Veronica Bowers, and Marie Sorenson. Sherman Dickman provided technical information for our troubleshooting section.

Hats off to Trygg Larsson-Danforth for kid-testing some of our ideas, Carlene Larsson for mom-testing them, Fred Danforth for dad-testing them, and Hazen Danforth for grandfather-testing them. A nice three-generational family computing effort!

Anna Botelho and Alyson Levine of CIS Graphic Communications in Cambridge, Massachusetts did a terrific job of designing the book and composing pages.

We're also grateful to our agents, Glen Hartley and Lynn Chu, for tending to the business side of the project.

Finally, we owe a great debt to our children, Noah and Audrey, who helped test many of our ideas and patiently waited while we hogged Kid Pix for ourselves.

ANNOUNCING THE GREAT KID PIX ACTIVITY CONTEST!

Have you or your child invented any Kid Pix™ activities of your own? If so, share them with us — you'll have a chance to win a free copy of the Kid Pix Companion™, the ideal enhancement for Kid Pix, complete with new stamps, coloring books, and zany animation features. Broderbund will award a copy of the Kid Pix Companion to the best entry for each of the seven categories in *The Official Kid Pix Activity Book* (Mind Challengers, Kid Pix Games, Fantasy and Imagination, Video Olympics, Screen Gems, Electronic Bookworks, and Kid Pix Printouts). As the authors of the book, we'll judge entries on the basis of creativity, ingenuity, skill-building content, and versatility for children of different ages. Although there will be one official winner for each category, EVERY-ONE who submits ideas stands to win; if we use your ideas in future editions of *The Official Kid Pix Activity Book*, we'll acknowledge and provide you with a free copy of the new book. We look forward to hearing from you!

How to Enter

To enter the contest, send us a description of your activity. Be sure to describe any variations that can be used to modify the activity for older or younger kids, groups of kids, and so on. If you have a print-out of any sample drawings related to the activity, include them (you can also send us a diskette, Mac or PC). Your entry should include the following information in addition to the description and sample artwork: Your name, your child's name and age, address, telephone number, and type of computer (Mac or PC). If you have a PC, please specify whether you're using the DOS or Windows version. *(See back of book for contest rules)*

Deadlines

All entries must be post-marked no later than December 31, 1993. Winners and alternates will be selected and prizes awarded within 60 days thereafter and prize winners will be notified by first class mail.

Where to send entries

Send your entries to: P.O. Box 1646, Cambridge, MA 02238

Contents

Introduction

When our publisher, Michael Mellin, first asked us to develop a series of family computing activity books, he knew that we would be challenged by the offer. We had previously published what turned out to be a runaway success called *365 TV-Free Activities You Can Do With Your Child*, and were pointing people *away* from video screens and towards each other. Now, we have nothing against computers, and use them regularly to produce our manuscripts, manage our finances, and the like. We've even been involved with teaching basic computer skills through tutorial books for the past ten years. But family computing, Michael? Seemed a bit much—wasn't this just a different kind of "electronic hearth" or "plug-in-drug?"

We were also concerned about family computing from a standpoint of content. We had looked at educational and entertainment software over the years, and concluded that many software games are no improvement over inane TV cartoons and violent programming (lots of blasting and zapping going on in the skies and galaxies). We also concluded that much of the educational software was no match for a good book, a pad and pencil, and, most importantly, an interested parent who had even a modicum of time.

When we discovered Kid Pix, though, we saw exciting new possibilities for family computing and eagerly agreed to take on the project. We were impressed by the program's ingenious design and the way that it enables children to create and manipulate images in ways that can't be done manually. We also quickly found that we could devise group activities that would allow us to *interact* as a family while we used the program—even our younger child, two and a half, got in on the action. (Our biggest gripe about television, aside from its stultifying effects and exposure to violence, is that it's "anti-interactive"—when people are tuned in to the tube, they're generally tuned out to each other.) So while we still focus on pencil, paper, crayons, and paints in our household, Kid Pix has become a highly valued tool in our repertoire of non-TV activities.

In this book, we've assembled a collection of ideas that we hope you and your children will enjoy, and that you can use to create your own quality family computing time. We invite you to send us feedback and any variations you can offer (see the contest announcement for more information), and we look forward to hearing from you!

What's Inside!

Before describing the contents of the activities in the following pages, we want to stress that this is not a "how-to-use-Kid Pix" book. While we do provide a crash course for the impatient in Appendix A, we recommend that you experiment with the program first and at least skim through the Broderbund manual. Kid Pix offers a rich variety of clever tools, many of which are used in our activities. As you'll discover, a number of the tools have surprising effects when you apply them to the drawing screen. By experimenting a bit with the tools, you'll get maximum enjoyment out of the program and this book.

We also urge you to read our hints for family computing (below) which will help you get the most enjoyment out of our Kid Pix activities. Using computers for family entertainment and education is not quite like playing other games—it doesn't take much to frustrate or bore your child, so you need to be aware of potential problems that can derail a well-intentioned activity session.

Finally, while you and your child will develop excellent mouse-maneuvering skills from doing our Kid Pix activities, be aware that this book is not a computer literacy book in disguise. You won't find any information about DOS prompts, Macintosh folders, hard disks, or the like (there are scads of books in the stores on basic computing).

What we do offer is a set of recipes for hours of fun and skill-building at your computer. Each of the seven chapters in the book contains sets of related activities that can be easily modified for children four to fourteen (bigger kids and adults will probably find lots of the activities fun, too). The activities can be done with you and one child or with groups of children. Here's a thumbnail sketch of what you can expect in the following pages:

Chapter 1: Mind Challengers

The activities in this chapter are designed to challenge your child's recall (*Memory Drawing* and *Memory Teasers*), his or her ability to find hidden patterns (*I See a Pattern*), decipher codes (*Code Busters*), and visualize the immediate environment in terms of maps and plans (*Cartography 101* and *Junior Architect*). Participants in these activities will find numerous opportunities to draw on their creativity and problem-solving abilities.

Chapter 2: Kid Pix Games

These activities use the various Kid Pix drawing tools for interactive play. You'll find a number of games that involve following clues (*Treasure Hunts*), creating drawings from "dictation" (*Take a Drawing*), uncovering hidden messages (*Secret Messages*), following visual clues (*Dot-to-Dot*), and other challenges. The games also encourage children to use their math and language skills.

Chapter 3: Fantasy & Imagination Games

In this chapter, you'll find a collection of activities that use Kid Pix to help your child stretch his or her mind beyond what's on the screen. For example, your child can use Kid Pix to "view" the heavens and invent new constellations (*Night Skies*), create scenes for travel brochures for imaginary places (*My Summer Vacation*), illustrate and visually interpret dreams (*Dreamscapes*), and design visual means for communicating with extraterrestrials (*Cosmic Messages*).

Chapter 4: Video Olympics

These activities use Kid Pix to develop your child's mouse dexterity and agility. One, for instance, requires your child to move the LEAKY PEN tool through a maze without oozing beyond the walls (*Amazing Mazes*). Another (*Obstacle Course*) also sets up a treacherous course that demands precision movement. And yet another (*Steady Hand*) builds your child's ability to draw lines on the straight and narrow.

Chapter 5: Screen Gems

The activities in this chapter provide a number of suggestions for using Kid Pix to enhance artistic and visual communication skills in unexpected ways, such as creating pictures with only a limited number of shapes (*Geometry Drawings*) or drawing by creating voids in a solid background (*Eraser Painting*). Other *Screen Gems* activities offer unusual drawing projects, such as creating a family coat of arms and logos for wacky products (*Great Logos*).

Chapter 6: Electronic Bookworks

These activities use Kid Pix to add a new dimension to story-making (*Story Illustrators*), create tall tales based on the built-in Kid Pix stamps (*Stamp Stories*), and create opportunities for family story-telling opportunities (*Build a Story*). Other activities explain how to make family vacation books and various documents that can be viewed on-screen or printed out, such as the electronic comic strip (*Kid Pix Funnies*).

Chapter 7: Kid Pix Printouts

The activities in this final chapter are designed to generate printouts that can be used for entertainment (*Flip Book*), as well as printouts that have practical use, such as *Small Press*, *Printed Matter*, and *Family Gazette*. They're fun to do and will draw on a variety of your child's Kid Pix skills.

A Note about Hardware

Chances are you won't have to modify your system or purchase any additional equipment to run Kid Pix or do our activities. Still, you should read the following equipment considerations:

Computers

The activities in this book can be used with Kid Pix's running on IBM or Macintosh computers. While Kid Pix is essentially the same for both types of computers, there are subtle differences, such as the way the keyboard is used to generate squares and circles, and control the size of the electronic picture stamps. We've noted the differences when they're relevant to our activities.

Monitors

We have made numerous suggestions for using color throughout this book. If you have a monochrome monitor, in many cases you can achieve the same effect by using different dot screens to give you shades of gray. With a handful of activities, however, such as those involving "secret messages," you must have a color monitor. Note that with IBM computers running DOS or Windows, the colors available for use in Kid Pix will depend on the circuit board that controls your monitor (called the "graphics adaptor"). Different adapters, as well as the way your computer is set up (especially if you're using Windows), will affect what you see on-screen. In some cases, you will have limited choices for activities involving secret message games.

Printers

With the exception of the activities in Chapter 7, a printer is not required to use this book. A small number of activities in other chapters, however, will be enhanced if you have a printer—printout suggestions are given where appropriate.

And a Note about Navigating through this Book

As you'll soon notice, each chapter begins with an illustration that includes family members hovering around a computer. The image on the computer screen symbolizes the kind of activities you'll find in the chapter and is duplicated on the tabs on the right hand pages. This should make it easy to thumb through the book and pick out activity categories that strike your or your child's fancy. The index also identifies activities designed for groups and parties, activities suited for older kids (eight to fourteen), activities suited for younger kids (four to seven), "quick studies" (activities that can be done with little or no preparation), and other useful categories.

Finally, you'll notice that some words, such as WACKY BRUSH, PAINT CAN, ERASER, and so on, appear in a special type font. This font is used to identify Kid Pix tools and tool options.

In Case of Difficulty

While we promised not to bog you down with computer terminology, we recognize that computers can be finicky, and you might have difficulty with the program. To help get you up and running, and possibly avoid a call to Broderbund, we've included the Kid Pix Problem-Solver in Appendix B. This troubleshooting guide, which we compiled with the help of our friends on Broderbund's technical support team, provides easy answers to the questions most frequently asked by Kid Pix Users. The Problem-Solver is divided into Mac and PC (DOS and Windows) sections.

Hints for Happy Family Computing

If you have Kid Pix up and running on your computer, you're all set to do the activities in this book. First, though, please take a moment to read through the following suggestions for getting the most out of your family computing sessions.

1. **Be Open-Minded.** The only rule that we have with regard to our Kid Pix activities is that there aren't any rules! (The very beauty of the computer is that it opens new avenues for creativity—don't limit them.) We'll often suggest an object or goal for an activity, but if your child has a more appealing way to get there, terrific! If he or she wants to change the object of the game itself, all the better!

   For instance, with *Take a Drawing*, you "dictate" shapes for your child to draw, and see if he or she can create an image that you have in mind. Let's say that your child gets excited about what he or she is creating and wants to add a few shapes of his or her own. As a result, the drawing may not at all resemble what you had envisioned. That's fine! You've used a Kid Pix activity to stimulate the creative process and have done so in an enjoyable way. What more could you want?

We think of our activities as springboards and catalysts for creative fun, so we encourage you to encourage you child to "have it his or her way." If our experience is any indication, once you give permission to open the "idea floodgates," you'll be deluged with creative variations that will occupy you and your child for as long as you like.

(Again, let us know what your child comes up with—see the contest announcement.)

2. **Adjust the Activities to Your Child's Age and Abilities.** You're far and away the best expert on your child and are therefore in the best position to decide what's an appropriate challenge. You'll quickly get a sense of what your child can and cannot do with a mouse, how many items he or she can remember when doing a memory game, and so on.

In many cases, we give specific information on making an activity easier or harder to do; in others, it's obvious how to adjust the challenge. This is important, because if an activity is too difficult, you'll quickly frustrate your child; if it's too easy, your child will just as quickly lose interest.

As a general guideline, with younger children, start off simple then increase the difficulty by small degrees; for older kids, you might want to start off with a level of play that you know will be on the easy side, then quickly escalate the difficulty—older kids will often respond to this kind of "sneaky" challenge.

For instance, with *Eagle Eye*, your child tries to detect how you've changed a picture while he or she faced the other way. Do something quite obvious for younger players; start off with but a few objects in your picture, then remove the largest and most colorful. With older kids, try the game with a moderately dense picture and choose something that would be obvious after a quick scan. Then, on the next round, pull out the stops and see if your child can notice extremely fine changes in the picture, such as a small circle that has been changed from black to gray, or a tiny object that has been moved from one portion of the screen to another.

Whatever your approach, we recommend that you play each activity on your own before sitting down at the screen with the family. Give some thought to the level of play that you'll introduce for each family member. Besides, you might not get much of a chance to play once your child starts doing the activities!

3. **"Quality," Not "Quantity," Is the Key.** These days, "quality time" has become a buzzword. But even so, there is a very real difference between sitting down half-focused on your child's play activities and being there 110 percent. (Your child has an incredibly accurate "presence detector" and knows exactly whether your mind is focused or straying during play.) Of course, time is precious, especially for working and single parents, and it's often hard to muster up euphoric energy when you'd really rather sit down, unwind, and recharge your batteries before getting into play.

The solution is to identify small blocks of time that you can devote to Kid Pix activities. Perhaps pick out several activities the evening before you go to work, then agree on a time when you'll sit down at the computer. Older kids might want to prepare some of the more complicated screens or surprise you on their own after school or after dinner while waiting for you to join the fun.

In any case, trite as it might sound, ten minutes of quality, focused time will mean more to your child than a half an hour of sitting at the screen with less than a full tank of enthusiasm.

4. **Curb Competitive Play When Possible.** There's plenty of time in life for kids to learn how to jockey for position or cross the finish line first. Why dampen family fun with winners and losers? While some activities in this book inherently require a winner, you can downplay the competitive implications by having people compete against their own previous scores rather than each other. Perhaps one of your children is the first to get 50 points on a certain activity, say *Blindfold Movers*, in which players take turns trying to move objects to a target—with their eyes closed. Cast the praise in terms of "Wow, that's the most you've ever gotten"! Then, be sure to jot down the event in a "family book of records."

Another way to defuse the competitive issue is to make the prize for being the "firstest," or getting the "mostest," the privilege of selecting the rules for the next game.

The competition issue will most likely raise itself when groups of children play the activity, especially when kids seven, eight, or nine years of age are involved. Competition at that age can become so ferocious that the participants stop enjoying the activity and focus on winning or losing. Stress the cooperative aspects of the activities and the personal challenges involved, and reinforce the idea that *everyone* is a winner when doing the activities.

5. **Select "Emergency" Activities for Rainy Days.** As you get a feel for which kinds of activities fit your child's interests and abilities, think about "tucking" some away for a rainy day. These might be variations on activities that have been a big hit, or activities that you'll hold out as "sanity-savers."

6. **Keep an Archive.** The majority of activities don't call for a printout, so you may likely just erase the screen or start from scratch when you move onto another game. If your child does something particularly interesting, be sure to save the file before starting a new activity. Over time, you'll have an interesting archive that reveals your child's evolving creations on the computer.

Finally, there's the issue of interaction. In an ideal world, we would all spend much more time with our children. But this isn't an ideal world, and we have our work and daily household responsibilities, as well as our need for personal time. Our kids need personal time, too. So while most of the activities assume interaction between parent and child, we have included some activities that your child can do on his or her own once you've explained the basics. You can then tend to household chores, fix dinner, relax, exercise, or finish work you've brought home. Later, when you do have time to interact, your child can show you his or her works of art and creativity.

However you do the activities, remember that the only real goal is to have fun. For as Mark Twain concluded, "A good and wholesome thing is a little harmless fun in this world. . . ." And what could be more fun (and wholesome) than goofing around with your kids using magical tools to paint the world anew?

Steve Bennett

Ruth Loetterle Bennett

If you would like to purchase a selection of illustrations from this book on diskette (Macintosh format only), please drop us a note at: P.O. Box 1646, Cambridge, MA 02238.

CHAPTER 1...

Mind Challengers

Eagle Eyes

C hildren often have remarkable abilities to remember minutiae (as well as promises you made weeks ago and haven't come through with yet). Here are two activities that will enable them to flex their "visual memory muscles." Yours, too!

1. What's Different?

To play this activity, you'll need to create a "junk" pile on the screen. First make sure your child isn't looking at the screen. Then create a screenful of random shapes, lines, wacky patterns, and so on. Sprinkle the scene with stamps. The more irregular and chaotic, the better. When the screen is nicely littered, have your child look at it for five or ten seconds, then close his or eyes or turn around. With the ERASE, remove or alter one of the shapes or stamps. You can also use the MOVING VAN to rearrange the screen. Then, have your child look at the screen, and identify what has changed. Be sure to take turns—your child will love creating a challenge for you.

When playing with younger children, keep the screen very simple, say, four to six items; for older kids (or fellow adults), go hog wild. For older children, try using the PAINT BRUSH to change the fill or add shading to an object. The MIXER, REVERSE OPTION is also a great way of making interesting differences. And if you have a hotshot teenager or spouse, test their mettle by creating a very complex screen "mess," then without altering it, ask, "What's different?" Ha!

Before　　　　*After*

How many differences can you detect?

2. Have a Blast!

As in the previous activity, create an arrangement of shapes and stamps on the screen, and save the file. Have your child study the screen, then ignite the FIRECRACKER (an option of the ERASER tool). When the screen clears, see if your child can recreate the original scene from memory (you can always recall the saved version to check it out later—you might also want to print it before setting off the FIRECRACKER. Gauge the complexity of the screen picture and the viewing time to your child's age and abilities. And be sure to experiment with the other ERASER options as well, such as SLIP SLIDING AWAY and FADE AWAY. Then, try your hand at recreating your child's screen arrangement. How far did you get?

Trees and Forests

Here's a set of activities that gives new meaning to the old expression, "can't see the forest for the trees." Each of these activities challenges you and your child to find objects, letters, and the like within a "forest" of screen clutter.

1. Hidden Letters, Numbers, and Words

First, lay down a collection of letters or numbers. For older children, write a few short sentences. (Don't let your child observe what you type on the screen.) Save your file. Now for the fun: Clutter the screen with distracting shapes and stamps. The PAINT CAN with its various textured backgrounds does a great job of obscuring your letters, numbers, and words. To really create visual havoc, use the ELECTRIC MIXER too, particularly the SPLASH and CHECKERBOARD options. When you're done, have your child see if he or she can find the hidden letters, or read the hidden words. (Open the original file to demonstrate what's really there.) Then switch roles, and try your own eyes at the game.

2. Camouflaged Stamps

This activity involves burying stamps amidst the screen clutter. The key to making the stamps hard to find is to strategically place them in areas of similar color, shape, and curvature. (Younger children will find it easier if you use larger stamps—press Shift when using the STAMP TOOL to increase the stamp size.) For added fun, your child can use

the WACKY PENCIL to draw a circle around each stamp he or she finds.

3. Mirror, Mirror...

Draw faces with the various WACKY PENCIL and WACKY BRUSH tools, save your file (for proof that there really is a face hiding in there), and mess up the screen with all of the Kid Pix tools at your disposal. Then, have your child or other family members find the fairest face on the screen. For sure, it's the one reflected on the blank screen!

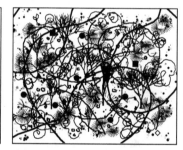

Before   *After*

I See a Pattern

During the final presidential debate of 1992, George Bush thought he could stage a surprise victory by pointing out his main opponent's pattern of flip-flopping on issues. Well, as history proved, being able to recognize patterns won't guarantee you a second term in the White House. But as these activities demonstrate, it will provide great fun for everyone in *your* house.

1. Alphanumeric Patterns

In this activity, you use letters and numbers to create patterns. For young children, stick with short, simple combinations, say, two or three repeating letters. See how many you can add and still have your child recognize the pattern. Then, turn the tables, and see how you do.

2. Stamp Patterns

In this variation, you use stamps to make repeating patterns. Again, keep it simple for young players, using easy combinations such as apple, clown, house, and so on. For older kids, create patterns that extend for multiple lines or even wrap around the screen.

3. Dots the Way It Goes

You can use the DOTS option of the WACKY BRUSH to lay down 20 or 30 clear dots that snake around the screen. (Each time you click, Kid Pix will generate a clear dot. Don't hold the button and drag the mouse—the program will generate a random pattern of clear and solid dots, defeating the purpose of the activity.) Now, create a pattern of 20 to 30 dots by darkening a sequence of the clear dots and then repeating the sequence one more time. Can your child identify the basic pattern?

4. Next in Line

This activity is a favorite in our household. The idea is to create a pattern, but on the second set, stop midway. Ask your child what comes next.

5. What's Wrong Here

Use any of the above suggestions for making a pattern. Repeat it once or twice, but also make an intentional mistake. Your child's mission: First figure out the pattern, then figure out the error. Double the action, double the fun!

Memory Drawing

"**M**emory is a painter," declared Grandma Moses. "It paints pictures of the past and of the day." True, but can you and your child paint by memory? Find out with these activities.

1. Quick Study

This activity requires one outside prop: a picture. You can use a photograph, a page of a magazine or book, a brochure, a piece of junk mail (a great way to put it to good use)—anything with an image. Show the picture to your child and place it out of view, then see if he or she can reconstruct the image from memory. For younger children, select something simple and familiar, and let them have a good long look. For older kids, up the challenge by selecting more complex images and only letting them view it briefly. Take turns so your child also can become the art selector. Besides, that way you get to have fun, too!

2. A Room with a View

This activity relies on the Kid Pix artist's memory and powers of observation. To play, your child looks around the room until you call out "Stop"! He or she then tries to recreate the scene (or part of it) on-screen. Adjust the "viewing" according to your child's age—younger children will require more time to "take it all in." For older kids, you can increase the challenge by deliberately putting something out of place, say, a couch pillow on top of a table. Or, move a lamp. Will your child draw the room as seen or as remembered? The answer will surely be interesting!

3. Sartorial Splendor

Quick. Without looking, do you remember what your child is wearing? Does your child remember what you're wearing? Find out by taking turns doing portraits of each other, without looking at anything but the screen. The two of you should try to capture colors, textures, or whatever you can remember. You might be surprised to learn that you're actually wearing snow shoes today!

Memory Teasers

I f you enjoyed the preceding *Memory Drawing* activities, you're sure to like these activities as well; they'll put your memory through the ultimate "mental obstacle course."

1. Memory Grid

First you'll need to prepare the "game board"—make sure your child isn't watching. Subdivide your screen into six compartments using the LINE tool and the Shift key (refer to the Introduction). Save the file—call it "GRID." Then, place a stamp from one of the palettes in each compartment on the screen. (You might want to double the size of the stamps by pressing Option on the Mac, and Ctrl on the PC. To triple the size, press Shift on the Mac, and Ctrl+Shift on the PC). Again, save the file. Now, have your child study the screen for a brief time before you clear it. Use the ERASER tool with the COUNT DOWN, SLIP SLIDING AWAY, FADE AWAY, or SWEEP options. Open the file called GRID, and ask your child to place the same stamps in the same compartments of the grid. (Save the file for comparing your child's grid with the original.)

You can adjust the difficulty of the activity by increasing or decreasing the number of compartments, by increasing or decreasing the number of stamp palettes you use when selecting stamps, and by shortening or lengthening the amount of time your child views the arrangement. (Experiment with the ERASE tool options to factor in how long it takes for the screen to clear.) Whiz kids may be

challenged by a grid of ten or twelve stamps, while younger kids may be more comfortable with six or less.

In any case, commend your child for the fine job he or she did with such a tough exercise. Just hope your kids are as kind when you try it yourself!

2. Memory Lane

This activity is a simple variation of *Memory Grid*, and is designed for young children. Instead of erasing the objects as you did in the *Memory Grid* activity, use the MOVING VAN to drag the stamps to a corner of the screen. (Be sure not to place them in the same order as they were on the grid.) Your child can then use the MOVING VAN to reposition them where he or she thinks they belong. This is certainly easier than remembering the stamps and searching the palettes for them. It's also a great way for young Kid Pix artists to get the hang of driving the MOVING VAN across the screen.

The Mind's Eye I

We usually associate drawing with seeing. But there are whole other levels of sensory and motor actions going on, too, when you do a Kid Pix drawing. These activities are meant to be done with the "mind's eye"—using Kid Pix without any visual cues. They're fun and will give your child new appreciation for the rich world of touch.

1. Freeform Drawing

This is the simplest kind of "mind's eye" activity; the artist announces what he or she intends to draw, then sets about doing so with his or her eyes closed. For starters, you or your child should select a drawing tool and place it on the drawing screen *before* closing your eyes; this will help keep the drawing on the screen and reduce the likelihood of moving the cursor into unwanted areas. In addition, you can select the Small Kids Mode from the Goodies menu— this prevents the cursor from causing problems if it goes off the drawing screen.

The better you and your child get at visualizing the drawing, the more you'll be able to keep the cursor on the drawing screen. Once you have the hang of drawing with the mind's eye, try selecting the drawing tools with your eyes closed as well. The results can be startling!

2. Left, Right, Left

A popular creativity exercise for getting people to open their minds involves having one person wear a blindfold

and another serve as a guide—gets interesting around issues like eating and navigating doorways. This activity extends the guide concept to the Kid Pix drawing screen. The artist closes his or her eyes, and the other person gives out instructions for moving the mouse, such as "up," "stop," "right," "down," "slow," and so on. When the guide says "Done," the artist tries to figure out what he or she has just drawn—without looking, of course.

Start off with simple shapes, then graduate to portraits, landscapes, and the like. As in the first activity, it can be quite jarring to the artist to rely on touch rather than vision to create a picture. But, when drawing with the mind's eye, everyone will be surprised at how sophisticated the images can be.

3. A Helping Hand

Rather than verbally guiding your child through a blindfold Kid Pix drawing, place your hand atop his or hers, and move the mouse. See if he or she can figure out what you're drawing by the mouse's motions. Try drawing numbers and letters, and writing out whole words (older kids). Perhaps you'll find that the hand really *is* quicker than the eye!

The Mind's Eye II

In the previous activities, the artist learned to use the mouse to create images without visual cues. In these activities, your child uses the mouse for precision action in a series of "high action" games. Your child will again find it different and challenging to use touch instead of sight to navigate across the drawing screen.

1. Pin the Tail on the...

Here's a way to play pin the tail on the donkey without the dangers of sharp pins. Have your child draw a donkey (or an elephant, dinosaur, or whatever) on the screen, as well as a separate (appropriate or inappropriate) tail. The players then take turns trying to use the MOVING VAN to affix the tail to the animal. It's easier to highlight the tail with your eyes open, then close your eyes as you move the mouse. Highly skilled tail-pinners may prefer to do the selecting and the moving by feel alone. Your kids might also want to play the game with inanimate objects—pin the wheel on the car, the propeller on the plane, or one of our favorites, the tooth on the Saber Tooth Tiger.

2. Blindfold Movers

This activity presents a rare opportunity to (legally) drive with your eyes closed. On one side of the screen, draw a set of concentric squares or circles—this is the target. The lines of the squares or circles should be about three quarters of an inch apart. Now, place a collection of stamps (perhaps all the vehicles) at the opposite side of the screen, about a quarter of an inch apart. The person using the

mouse selects the MOVING VAN and highlights one of the stamps, then closes his or her eyes and tries to drag one of the stamps into the center of the target. You can assign different values to each zone (indicated by numbers, letters, colors, fills, etc.), with some being positive and others negative. Older kids can invent intricate scoring systems with positive and negative points.

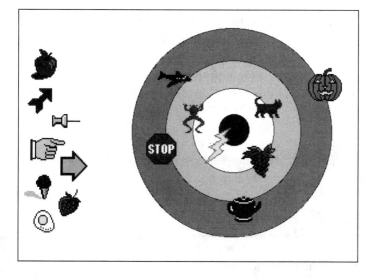

Alternatively, your child can lay down several adjacent boxes, rectangles, ovals, or other shapes. The object of the game is to drag the stamps to specific shapes. Develop a scoring system of your child's choosing. Whether you play with one child or ten, the action is sure to cause plenty of laughs.

Jigsaw Puzzle

S o you're pretty good at assembling those thousand-piece jigsaw puzzles of solid blue skies, eh? Try your hand at some electronic versions. No, they probably won't contain a thousand pieces, but you'll certainly find them an entertaining challenge.

1. Easy Jigsaw

This activity is ideal for younger kids. With your child in another room or facing the other direction, create a simple picture on the drawing screen using the WACKY PENCIL and a medium point. Choose something common, like an animal, a person, a house, a favorite toy, and so on. Then, use the MOVING VAN tool and its options to move pieces of the picture around the screen. Leave plenty of room around the pieces so that your child can use the MOVING VAN to reassemble the pieces. Hmm, that tail *could* actually make a good rhinoceros horn. . . .

2. Scramble Puzzle

This activity requires more dexterity—in fact, you can make it quite a challenge for older kids and grownups alike. Draw a vertical line about a third of the way from the left or right side of the screen. Make a drawing on the larger portion of the screen. Then, fill in the background on the large portion with the PAINT CAN. Next, subdivide the drawing into equal, rectangular, or square compartments by using the LINE tool with the Shift key to draw vertical and horizontal lines. Finally, use the MOVING VAN'S MAGNET option to rearrange the compartments. Use the blank third

of the screen as a "holding" area while you're rearranging the drawing. When you're done, invite your child to use the MAGNET to restore the picture.

Before   *After*

3. Geometry Puzzle

Create a solid rectangle, square, triangle, or circle, and chop it up with the MOVING VAN. Then, see if your child can use the VAN to reassemble it. Note: You'll have to tell younger kids what the shape is before they try to re-assemble it. For older kids, increase the difficulty by making them figure out the shape as well as what goes where. And for the ultimate challenge, chop up several geometrical shapes, and let your expert puzzle-solver put all of them back together!

Junior Architect

Is your child a budding architect? Find out with these Kid Pix activities. They suggest ways for your child to draw simple floor plans and at the same time demonstrate his or her grasp of spatial relationships. There's a fringe benefit here as well: In ten or fifteen years, you might get a discount when you need a design for that new addition to your den.

1. My Room

This activity helps the Kid Pix artist to get a "satellite's eye view" of the interior of your house. Have your child draw a square or rectangle representing his or her room, then draw the main objects in their proper places. For younger children, just ask where their bed and dresser are located. Older kids can show doorways, light fixtures, and so on.

Once your child has his or her room on the screen, suggest using the MOVING VAN to do a little rearranging. Perhaps swap the furniture, or create a new doorway or windows. Or perhaps even use the VAN to straighten the piles of junk covering the floor—it might be the easiest time you've ever had getting your child to clean up his or her room.

2. My House

Once your child has the hang of depicting his or her room, move onto other rooms on the same floor. Suggest that advanced architects create mini-plans on the drawing screen for all floors of the house. Then, do a little reconnaissance to check out the accuracy—you might be sur-

prised to learn that your bathroom is located in the middle of what you thought was the living room.

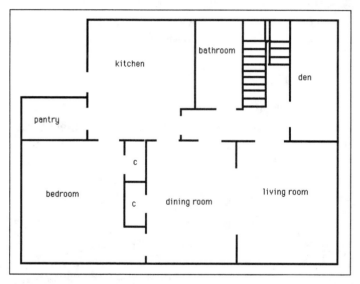

3. My Building

Do another floor plan for a familiar building, such as the library, school, bank, or supermarket. Check out the accuracy next time you visit the building. Perhaps your child can use the MOVING VAN option to create a better layout. In the supermarket, for example, wouldn't it make more sense to have the snacks and desserts all together near the door? That way, one could do the essential shopping, and skip the rest!

Cartography 101

Many children love the idea of maps, even if they don't fully understand them. These activities use Kid Pix to help your child create simple maps based on personal experience. They're fun to make and tie into your child's "local knowledge."

1. My Yard

With this activity, your child draws a map of your backyard, based on memory. (If you live in an apartment building, your parking lot or nearby sidewalks can become the subject of the map.) Suggest that your child work with key landmarks, like the big willow tree, the white picket fence, the garden, and so on.

Also suggest the use of color and fill patterns with the PAINT CAN to designate areas such as the lawn, flower beds, and driveway. Your child can use the LOOPER and PINE NEEDLES options to indicate trees and shrubs. Encourage the use of other WACKY BRUSH options or STAMPS to create plant life, too. (True jokers might suggest using the DOG stamp to represent dogwood trees!)

2. My Neighborhood

While younger children will have their hands full trying to draw a map of your backyard, older kids may well have enough of a sense of the neighborhood to draw a map. Suggest that the junior cartographers keep it simple, just focusing on major landmarks such as the playground, shopping area, public parks, friends' houses, and so on.

Don't forget to ask where your house fits into the grand
scheme of things!

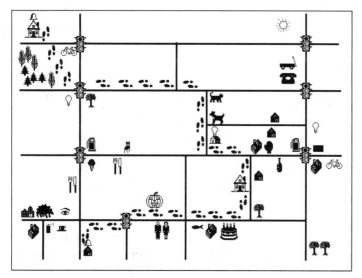

3. My City

Are you ready to visit the city, if only on paper? See if
your children can recreate the general layout of your city
(showing some of the prominent buildings). Older kids
might even be able to show you some streets, and perhaps
draw a map for a visitor of how to get to your house via
public transportation, or from the train station, airport,
highway, and so on. In any case, be sure to test out your
child's map—preferably with a visit to a favorite park or
playground!

Code Busters

K *RPPX*. No, we're not experiencing keyboard difficulties. We've just communicated an important message using a code. Kid Pix is great for creating visual codes that young children can readily understand. You can even gin up codes that will challenge the best math whiz in your house!

1. Alphabet Codes

With this activity, each letter of the alphabet gets replaced by another letter, number, or stamp (stamp codes are especially easy for younger kids to understand). Enter text from the keyboard (the Text plus the Option key on the Mac or the Ctrl key on the PC) or use the TEXT tool to place the letters on the screen. Next to or below each letter on the screen, stamp out a letter, number, or picture. Now, write a message in the code language you just created. See if your child can decipher it. Then, turn the tables, and see if you can decode a message in a code that your child devises. Happy decoding!

2. Hotshot Decoders

If your older child found the alphabet substitution code
activity too easy, try this variation. (It's also great at parties
for grownups!) Instead of listing all the alphabet letters, just
give replacements for the most commonly used letters in the
English language (in order of decreasing frequency, they are
E, T, A, O, N, R, I, S, and H). See if this is enough information to decipher the message. You can reveal these substitutions and additional replacements in other files—see how
few files your child needs to open in order to crack the code.

3. Electronic Morse Code

Morse Code may seem anachronistic in this computer age
(it was invented in the 1830s), but it's easy for kids to learn
and fun to do with Kid Pix. The code consists of dots and
dashes that stand for short and long sounds. Your child can
use a zero or a one, two letters, two stamps, and so on, as
substitutes. Don't be surprised if you hear tapping from
your child's bedroom tonight—the message might be,
"Guess who's still awake!"

A • −	J • − − −	S • • •	2 • • − − −
B − • • •	K − • −	T −	3 • • • −
C − • − •	L • − • •	U • • −	4 • • • • −
D − • •	M − −	V • • • −	5 • • • • •
E •	N − •	W • − −	6 − • • • •
F • • − •	O − − −	X − • • −	7 − − • • •
G − − •	P • − − •	Y − • − −	8 − − − • •
H • • • •	Q − − • −	Z − − • •	9 − − − − •
I • •	R • − •	1 • − − − −	0 − − − − −

CHAPTER 2...

Kid Pix Games

Take a Drawing

Have you ever dictated a letter or been on the other side of the pencil? If so, these activities will jog your memory banks—but with a twist. One person "dictates" the components of a drawing, while another, the "electronic scribe," tries to create the picture on the screen. The results can be quite surprising!

1. The Wheels on the Bus

Think of an object, say, a bus, then reduce it to a set of geometrical shapes for your child. You might say, "Draw a large rectangle, and place two circles along one side. Then, draw ten small squares in a row inside the rectangle. Use the PAINT CAN to color the rectangle yellow and the circles black." Compare what you had in mind with your artist's creation—and enjoy the differences! (A child we know drew the shape and identified it as an owl wearing a zippered jacket! For sure, "correctness" with this activity is "owl" in the mind of the mouse-holder.)

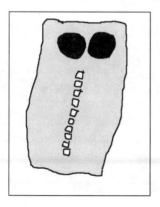

2. Three-for-All

Two might be company, but three's a good drawing crowd.
At least for this activity. In this variation on *The Wheels on
the Bus*, two children take turns adding features to the
drawing. (You can also do this activity in "team" fashion,
with each team conferring about the placement of various
shapes.) The more, the merrier—and the greater the
chances of drawing the unexpected!

3. Free for All

Here's yet another variation of *The Wheels on the Bus*.
Without seeing the screen, players call out random shapes;
the electronic scribe then draws and connects the shapes
at his or her discretion. When the scribe declares that a
recognizable object (or scene) is complete, the artwork is
revealed. Then, another player takes over the drawing, and
the play continues.

4. Grab that Pencil!

Rather than calling out geometrical shapes and directions,
try calling out Kid Pix tools, such as RED, WACKY BRUSH, and
PIES. Then, perhaps PAINT CAN, BLUE, and so on. Call out
"stop," and see how many recognizable items you and
your child can identify. (Groups can take turns calling out
tools.) Hmm, that does look like an octopus wearing a top
hat, do you think?

Finish that Pix!

I t's one thing to create a masterpiece from a blank screen. But it's quite another if you have to start with, say, two circles, three triangles, and four lines. Or, with a picture of a dinosaur, a helicopter, and a telephone. What could you and your child create from such unusual beginnings? These activities will test your creativity and provide a few chuckles as well.

1. Sticks and Stones - Basic

The "starter" places one or more lines, boxes, or other shapes on the drawing screen. The "finisher" must then use all of the elements on the screen as part of a recognizable object. Two vertical lines, for example, might become the walls of a house or the trunks of two trees in a landscape. Take turns being the "starter" and the "finisher."

The activity is especially well-suited to younger children; if they can get *anything* on the screen, you or an older sibling can then complete the drawing (which is bound to delight even the youngest kids).

2. Sticks and Stones - Advanced

The basic principle of this activity is the same as the first, but the idea is for the starter to use drawing elements that will require a more creative response from the finisher. For example, use the WACKY BRUSH to create pies, echoes, zig zags, and the like. For an added challenge, let the starter decide the category of the object to be drawn (animals, dinosaurs, fish, people, vehicles, buildings, food, etc.).

3. Create a Scene

Whereas *Sticks and Stones* used Kid Pix drawing tools, this activity entails using images from the stamp collections. The starter places a variety of stamps on the screen—the more incongruous the better! The finisher must somehow link the stamps together. Decide ahead of time whether the finisher is allowed to move the stamps, or whether he or she must create the scene around them. You'll be surprised at how even the strangest ensemble of things can be woven together into a delightful picture.

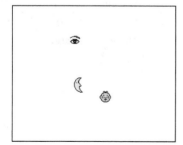

Grid Games

H ere's a set of activities that will sharpen your child's powers of observation around the house. You might even discover some very unusual items you never even knew resided under your roof.

1. Color and Wacky Brush Grid

Make a grid six squares by six squares using the LINE tool and the Shift key. (The Shift key ensures that your lines will be straight.) Place up to six dabs or swatches of color along the top. On the left side, place up to six different WACKY BRUSH strokes, such as BUBBLY, NORTHERN LIGHTS, or PIES.

When you finish the grid, it's time to play the game. The first player uses the ROLL-THE-DICE option of WACKY BRUSH (which creates random die "rolls" each time you click the mouse). The first roll indicates the horizontal position on the grid (the color swatch), while the second designates the vertical position. (This is a good counting exercise for your child.)

Let's say that a roll of five and three landed the player at the intersection of Green and Northern Lights (which makes lots of parallel lines). The player then gets up and searches the house for an item that is both green and has lots of parallel lines—like a comb or plastic fork from a takeout. Or a box of spinach linguini!

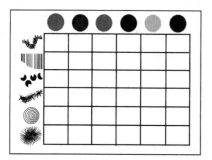

2. Color and Letter Grid

To do this activity, you'll need a grid as in the previous game. But instead of combining WACKY BRUSH options with colors, the idea is make a grid of colors and letters. If someone "rolls" a "blue F," he or she must search the house for something that has a blue F on it (a label, book, T-shirt, etc.). Any ideas for a "red Q"?

3. Color and Shapes Grid

Again, create a grid. But place shapes from the WACKY BRUSH, SHAPES AND MORE SHAPES option on the left side instead of the letters. Each time you click on the mouse button, one of five geometrical shapes will appear. If you get a duplicate shape, use UNDO MAN to eliminate it until a different shape appears. Each player then "rolls" the die as above, and looks for objects around the house with the specified color and shape. "Sure," you're probably thinking. "Where can I find a yellow hexagon?" Answer: in your pencil drawer!

Dot-to-Dot

I f you've been to a family restaurant with your kids, you've no doubt encountered dot-to-dot games and the like on place mats. Here are some activities that will enable your child to use Kid Pix to play his or her own dot-to-dot games—and you won't have to spring for a meal while they're at it.

1. Do-It-Yourself Dot-to-Dot

This activity is geared toward younger kids who can't read double-digit numbers yet. Make a drawing using the WACKY PENCIL, then erase long segments, leaving very short segments for the "dots." Label the dots with numbers from one to ten (use the TEXT tool, third palette). Then, have your young Kid Pix artist connect the dots with the WACKY PENCIL. For kids who know their ABC's, you can use alphabet letters instead.

2. Automatic Dot-to-Dot

Kid Pix contains a built-in dot-to-dot generator, located on the second palette of the WACKY BRUSH. Just hold the mouse and draw, and the program will generate a fine line connected by numbered dots. Move the mouse very quickly, or else the numbers will pile up on each other. When you lift your finger from the mouse, the connecting lines will disappear.

Another technique is to first make a drawing using the finest pencil point and a light color, then switch to the DOT TO DOT option and a darker color. Instead of holding down the mouse button, click every time you want a dot (when you apply dots one at a time this way, Kid Pix doesn't draw any connecting lines). The advantage is that you can place individual dots exactly where you want them and draw at a slower pace without being in the "dark." When you're done placing the dots, use the PAINT BUCKET to apply a background the same color as the line you drew. The lines will become invisible as they blend in with the background. Finally, change the PAINT BUCKET to white, and you'll have a clean background and a perfect dot drawing.

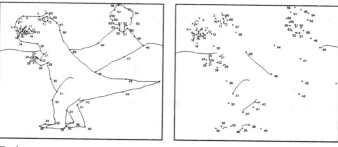

Before   *After*

3. Zen Dot-to-Dot

See if your kid can figure out a dot-to-dot drawing without actually filling in the lines—by just meditating on it.

Secret Messages I

Did you ever play with disappearing ink when you were a kid? If not, here's your big chance to relive a missing part of your childhood. And without the mess. By using various Kid Pix color and tool options, you can create hidden messages sure to amaze your child. This basic training in secret message writing is not only fun to do, but will enable you to do other activities in the book (see *Secret Messages II* and *Treasure Hunt*).

1. Stealth Technology

Just as the stealth aircraft is designed to evade enemy radar, the stealth message evades the gaze of the casual viewer. To create a hidden message, first examine your color palette and select the closest (most indistinguishable) pair of adjacent colors. Select the lighter of the pair, then choose the thinnest line option of the WACKY PENCIL. Write your message on the drawing screen, being careful not to enclose any spaces within letters such as *o*, *p*, and *d*. Next, return to the color palette, and select the darker of the pair of colors you identified earlier. Finally, use the PAINT CAN to fill in the background with the darker color. Magic! The message disappears (actually, it's just masked by the only slightly darker shade). Note: You'll have to apply the PAINT CAN to any interiors of letters you might have enclosed accidentally.

There are many ways to uncover your hidden message. One of the more interesting ones is the NIGHT AND DAY option of the ELECTRIC MIXER which inverts the colors on the whole screen in one fell swoop so that the lighter writing becomes dark, and the background becomes light. The HIGHLIGHT option of the ELECTRIC MIXER outlines every line on the screen, no matter how faint. The OUTLINER option works in a similar fashion. Finally, there's the QUESTION MARK option of the LINE tool, which inverts any colors that it sweeps over.

Try a few secret messages yourself; experiment with color combinations that work best on your computer. Your child will not only find it entertaining, but you'll develop a repertoire of secret message "deciphering" techniques that you can use in other activities in this book.

Secret Messages II

I f you enjoyed the "stealth technology" we introduced in the previous activity, try the advanced techniques in these activities—they open the door for all sorts of interesting games.

1. Find that Message

Create a message or draw a picture using the technique described on page 34. Then, have your child "decipher" the message or picture by using the INVERT option of the WACKY BRUSH (the WASH option of the WACKY PENCIL works well, too). As he or she moves the brush around, Kid Pix will invert the color of everything in the brush's path. Use a timer, and see if your child can reveal all of the hidden messages and pictures on your screen within, say, a minute or less (adjust to make age-appropriate). If your older child or spouse thinks it's too easy, toss in a few decoys—that ought to humble them a bit!

2. Guess that Message

In this activity, use the WACKY BRUSH as described above. The idea, though, is to see who can guess the nature of the message or image with the *least* portion of it uncovered.

3. Message Detectives

In addition to revealing hidden messages by inverting the backgrounds manually, you can deploy a variety of Kid Pix tool options for interesting special effects. For example, the ELECTRIC MIXER with the BROKEN GLASS option inverts portions of the screen randomly; with repeated applications, you can piece together a whole message or picture. What's the least number of applications your child needs to read your message?

4. Sherlock Holmes Approach

Another interesting tool for uncovering hidden messages is the ZOOM IN option of the ELECTRIC MIXER, which magnifies portions of the screen. If you keep your finger down on the mouse and move it across the screen, you can enlarge the lines enough to make them visible—in pieces, since the image is enlarged. You can also enlarge the hidden writing by using the MAGNIFYING GLASS option of the WACKY BRUSH. Well, Watson, what is it?

Treasure Hunts

I f you've been practicing your secret messages and codes, you can either apply for a job at the CIA or try something really adventurous, like the following activity. It's sure to bring high action excitement to your living room.

1. The Search for Buried Treasure

This activity combines several childhood favorites into one action game—finding secret messages, breaking codes, and going on treasure hunts. Here's how it works. Choose five or so hiding places in the house, and write secret or coded messages (see *Secret Messages I*, page 34 or *Code Busters*, page 22) directing your child to each location. Save each message in a different file.

At each hiding place, you will need to leave a message written on paper, giving a computer file name that contains the next message. Your child must decode or reveal the message in that file, using the code substitutions given or the WACKY BRUSH deciphering technique described in activity #1 of *Secret Messages II*, page 36. The computer message then directs the treasure-hunter to the next hiding place. This process continues until a final secret message directs him or her to the "treasure" (snacks are as good as gold).

For prereaders, the hunt can be done with secret message pictures. For younger readers, keep the written code or secret message simple. And with older kids, you can devise cryptic clues such as "northwest, parlor, orange, 223" (which could mean, go to the bookshelf in the living room, and look at page 223 of an orange book).

2. Three's a Party

You can easily adapt the hunt for groups of kids, too (great for birthday parties). Create coded or secret messages for each child participating in the hunt. Make the child's name part of the file names (such as David1, Claire2, etc.). The messages guide the players to separate places to find paper clues.

3. The Alpha Team

An alternative way to play with a group is to have a single electronic clue for each child. The electronic clues lead the children to paper codes that reveal different portions of the alphabet and their corresponding substitutions. When all the children have found their paper clues, they convene at the computer and work together to decode a final screen message that directs them to the treasure—perhaps the birthday cake itself!

Hiding Games

Here are two more activities that draw on *Code Busters* (page 22) and *Secret Messages II* (page 36). Both games involve action away from the computer as well as at the keyboard. Get set for a bustling time!

1. Mission Impossible

This activity involves having your child locate an object that you've hidden somewhere in the house. The key to the location lies in a secret message or code that you create prior to playing the game. Your child must find the message with the WACKY PENCIL deciphering technique (see *Secret Messages II*), or decode the message as in *Code Busters*. The message itself should be cryptic with regard to the object to be found and its location.

You can spice up the game by putting a time limit on how long a message or code may be viewed (use the various timed ERASE options to wipe the screen clean (see *Speed Readers*, page 96, for more details). You can also specify the amount of time that your child has to locate the hidden object. How much time will your child give you to find "something small and green somewhere in the house"?

2. Hide-and-Seek

Here's an electronic version of an age-old game for groups of children. Write secret messages that indicate a safe hiding spot in your house, as well as a "master list" revealing each hiding place in cryptic form ("under something warm and blue"—"a bed with a blue blanket"). Save each message as a separate file with the player's name. One by one, each child opens his or her file and deciphers the hidden message, then goes to the designated spot. The last child must then find the "hiders," using the clues, and bring everybody back for another round.

A separate variation entails having everyone take turns deciphering or decoding the same message, which sends them to one large hiding place. (This is called "Sardine Hide-and-Seek.") The hardest part isn't for the "seeker"; the hiders must keep from giggling while the last child roams the house!

Old Favorites

Here are two traditional games that you can play on the Kid Pix drawing screen. They both involve the use of the MOVING VAN to do things that would normally be done by hand. Kind of a "bionic" approach to old standbys.

1. Dominoes

Use the WACKY BRUSH, ROLL-THE-DICE option (second palette) to draw at least ten pairs of dice, or "dominoes," on the left side of the screen. Each time you press the mouse button, a die or half a domino will appear on the screen. Now, have your child use the MOVING VAN to transport one of the pairs, or a domino, to the right side of the screen. The idea is to find another domino on the left side of the screen whose number matches one of the ends of the dominoes placed on the right. Move the matching domino to the right side of the screen beside the previously placed dominoes. Take turns using the MOVING VAN until all of the dominoes are paired up, then try it again with more dominoes. How much of the screen can you fill?

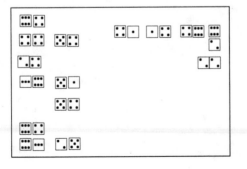

2. Tic Tac Toe

Create a grid with nine compartments, using the LINE tool and Shift key. Save the grid for future games. You and your child select X's and O's from the TEXT tool options—just plop your X or O where you want it on the grid. You can also create a stockpile of X's and O's, and place it to the side of the grid before you save it, or copy your X's and O's with the MOVING VAN (use the Option key, Mac, or Ctrl key, PC, when using the MOVING VAN). This will eliminate the need to continually dip in the alphabet palette when you want to make a move. Alternatively, select stamps to represent the X's and O's—frogs and cats, or ladybugs and lobsters, might be more interesting than letters.

When one person wins, use the LINE tool and Shift key to draw the winning row or diagonal. Another way to play the game is to let Kid Pix generate the X's and O's with the LOTS OF HUGS AND X'S option of the WACKY BRUSH. Point the brush to an open grid compartment and click on the mouse—you'll either get an X or an O—you never know!

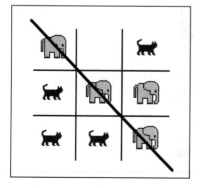

More Old Favorites

H ere are two more board games that take advantage of Kid Pix's MOVING VAN. The first is an electronic version of the old standby, checkers. The second is a word game that will appeal to any child who has reading skills.

1. Checkers

Create an eight squares by eight squares grid using the LINE tool and the Shift key. Use the PAINT BUCKET to darken alternating squares with whatever color strikes your child's fancy. Save your drawing. Select two stamps (say, strawberries and stop signs), and print out twelve of each on the screen in their white square starting positions (let each player choose the stamp for his or her pieces). The players use the MOVING VAN to move pieces and make plays on the board. Captured players are moved to the side of the board. And kings are created by restamping the square and using the Option key (Mac) or Ctrl key (PC) to create a larger version. May the best stamp win!

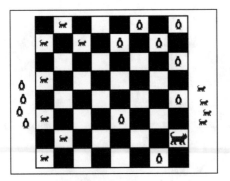

2. Word Games

Create a grid with as many compartments as will fit on your screen (use the LINE tool and Shift key to create straight lines). The compartments must be large enough to accommodate the TEXT tool letters. Save the grid before you start playing so you can use it again for future games.

One way to play is cooperatively, without points. A person spells a word with letters from the TEXT option palettes. The next person then adds another word that uses one of the letters in the word already on the screen. The object is to continue in this fashion, and fill up as much of the grid as possible—without scheming against one another.

You can also create a point system, assigning different values to different letters and coloring in certain squares that would have multiplier effects. You could still take a cooperative tact—the idea might be to jointly score as many points as possible for the family team.

Works-in-Progress

We all appreciate our kids' artwork when it's finished. Why not "eavesdrop" on a work-in-progress? These activities turn the "eavesdropping" process into mystery games in which you try to anticipate your child's final masterpiece.

1. What's My Line

No, this activity isn't about occupations; the idea is for one or more observers to guess what the artist is creating on-screen while the work is in progress. The Kid Pix artist stops at various points and asks if anyone can determine what the final piece will look like. Let's see—the Eiffel Tower, right?

2. Bits and Pieces

This activity is a variation on "What's My Line." The idea is for the artist to create a drawing in disconnected segments, then see if other people can put it together in their minds, and guess the object. You and your child can alternate being the artist and the "guesser," or with a group of kids, who-ever figures out the picture first gets to draw the next picture.

3. Scrambled Kid Pix

Does your child enjoy putting jigsaw puzzles together? Here's a kind of "reverse jigsaw puzzle" activity that will challenge and amuse everyone who does it. Explain to your child that he or she needs to draw a picture with distinct elements (a house, a tree, a car, people, etc.), then save the file or create a printout. No peeking! Once the picture is drawn, and you've had a minute to study it, and then look away again, the idea is for your child to use the MOVING VAN or the MAGNET option to rearrange the screen (to use the moving tools, he or she will have to leave enough space between the elements; otherwise, it will be difficult to make "surgical" incisions in the drawing).

Once your Kid Pix artist has rearranged the screen enough to make it a challenging reassembly job, it's up to you to put it all back together. When you've taken your best shot, compare your rendition to the original file. How did you do? Switch places and create a scrambled picture for your child—and watch a real pro at work!

Before Scrambling

After Scrambling

CHAPTER 3...

Fantasy and Imagination Games

Rorschach Blots

I t's amazing how two people can look at the same
Rorschach blot and see two totally different things. The
same holds for Kids Pix screens—you can create color
and shape "blots," and have your family members com-
ment on what they see. The differing perceptions can be
quite amusing!

1. Indoor Cloud-Watching

Wouldn't it be nice to lie back on the grass, and do some
old fashioned cloud-watching? Well, perhaps you don't
have a lawn, you're in the middle of a monsoon, or the
grass is frozen stiff from a recent cold snap. From the com-
fort of your living room, you can do some indoor cloud-
watching with Kid Pix. Use the PAINT BUCKET to apply a sky
blue color to your screen (use black, or a dense dot screen
on a monochrome system), then select the WACKY PENCIL
and the largest, rounded point. Choose white as the color,
then close your eyes, and spray a random pattern (best to
shift into Small Kids Mode first). Presto! Instant "clouds."

Save your sky file, then have your child study the clouds
and use a fine pencil point with a contrasting color to outline any images he or she sees.

Save the file, then you and other family members can
take turns opening the blank sky file and identifying faces,
animals, and whatever things appear on the screen. Save
those files as well.

Finally, open up each of the files, and compare the images.
If you have a printer, print out the drawings and hold them

up side by side, and note the similarities and differences. You can use the printouts as part of a "shuffle story" (see chapter 7), in which you rearrange images and story lines for unlimited fun.

2. Name that Blob!

Here's another kind of Rorschach activity. Instead of painting skies and clouds, create a random arrangement of geometrical shapes as well as irregular blobs of colors or shades of gray. Use the various WACKY PEN options to coat the screen with interesting shapes—the LEAKY PEN, DOTS, BUBBLY, and SPLATTER PAINT options are especially good for that job. So is the SPLASH option of the ELECTRIC MIXER tool. Take turns pointing out the faces, objects, and animals each of you sees on the screen. The chartreuse gorilla eating the purple banana? Yep, he's right there in the center!

Great Chefs

K ids might not like to eat everything on their plates, but most enjoy cooking. What would your child serve up in a kitchen where anything is possible? Find out with these zany culinary activities.

1. Pizza with Pizazz

We hope that your computer doesn't get hot enough to bake pizza dough. But your child can make the screen sizzle with some great pizza fixings. All he or she has to do is press Shift while using the OVAL tool, and Kid Pix will create a perfect circle of any color from your palette. Add a layer of tomato sauce (an orange dot fill), then top with cheese (use the WACKY BRUSH, PINE NEEDLES option plus the Option key, Mac, or the Ctrl key, PC, to spread a generous helping of yellow mozzarella. The pizza chef/artist then takes "orders" for toppings from other family members. Use the WACKY BRUSH to create spices, various vegetables, pepperoni, and yes, even some hairy anchovies! The next person cleans the oven with the FIRECRACKER option and begins shaping another household favorite.

2. Full Course Meal

If you've whetted everyone's appetite with the pizza-making activity, let your child try his or her hand at serving a full course meal. The chef/artist sets an elegant table, complete with a decorative plate and silverware. He or she draws in the various courses, which family members then try to identify as they "clean" their plates with the ERASER tool. Sorry, that was the salt shaker you just ate, not a piece of cake.

3. Chef's Surprise

Here's a true challenge for any chef worth his or her salt. One person creates a collection of different colored shapes and textures on the screen. The next one must combine the available "food stuffs" and serve up a plate with names for the resulting sumptuous dishes.

4. Marvelous Mudpies

Create some circles, and color them appropriately. Add natural garnishes, such as grass clippings (using the PINE NEEDLES option of the WACKY BRUSH). Add some pebbles de jour (use the WACKY BRUSH, DOTS option), and some morning dew delight (WACKY BRUSH, DRIPPY PAINT option). Be sure to serve with a fresh glass of mud puddle.

Haute Couture

W hat will the jet set wear next season? Put your family fashion designer to work on the new line. With Kid Pix's dazzling tools, your designer prodigy will have all of Paris buzzing with excitement.

1. Designer Kids

Have your child paint a screen with the WACKY PENCIL, WACKY BRUSH, STAMP, OVAL, RECTANGLE, and LINE tools, then add fancy colors with the PAINT CAN. Next, suggest the use of the ELECTRIC MIXER tool options to jumble the screen. Congratulations, your child has just created a piece of wild-looking "fabric." Now, your junior designer can use the ERASER tools to "cut" the fabric into clothing ensembles. (Your child can also select white from the color palette and use the one of the finer points of the WACKY PENCIL to cut the cloth.) Finally, suggest the use of the WACKY BRUSH to create some attractive head attire.

2. Practical Threads

Wouldn't it be great for kids if someone invented an all-purpose suit that would include rain gear, mud gear, snow gear, sun gear, and the like? See what your child can come up with—perhaps even a pouch for a collapsible fishing rod in the event that a freak rainstorm causes the backyard to break off from the continent and float away!

3. One-Style-Fits-All

Women's business clothing is a mirror image of menswear—jackets, belts, vests, and even ties. Why shouldn't things go the other way, too? Let your child design the first truly egalitarian business wear. Or maybe take some cues from children's wear. How about some "Chairman Dentons"?

4. Martian Modern

What do Martians wear to formal dinner parties? Find out when your child draws a complete ensemble, including guadraophone head gear, double zipper "anti-grav" boots, and some *very* cool gill covers.

Advertising Moguls

D o you skip most of the advertisements you read in magazines and newspapers? Do you leave the room when commercials air on your television? Here are some ads that are sure to grab people by the lapels and rattle their teeth. Fortunately for the populace's dental health, the only place you'll see them is on your own computer screen.

1. Junior Ad Designer

Younger and older children alike can become advertising moguls using Kid Pix's collection of tools—you just have to plant the seeds of an idea in their minds. First, though, let your kids get the idea of what goes into an ad in terms of images and text. For that purpose, you have a great teaching tool right in your house—just clip advertisements from newspapers and magazines. (Hey, why not take advantage of all the money that the advertisers spent on Madison Avenue?) See if they can make replicas of the ads. (Choose your subjects wisely!) Younger kids can just place images on the screen, while older kids might want to experiment with copy. The ads will make for interesting art pieces. And they'll pave the way for doing the following creative activities.

2. Thirst Busters

Which beverage, in your child's opinion, is the real thing? You and your child can invent a cola or fizzy water product and then design the definitive on-screen ad that will put an end to the soft drink or bottled waters wars once and for all!

3. Wild Product Combos

Isn't the world just waiting for someone to invent a combination mouthwash and low-cal garlic salad dressing? Your
child's ad for such a product will no doubt stun the con-
suming public—"Finally, the taste of garlic without bad
breath!" What other wild combinations can your child
dream up and sell through the powers of advertising?

4. Your Kids' Toys

What's so special about your child's favorite toy, stuffed
animal, or doll? You'll find out when he or she designs
an ad for it! Encourage your child to describe its most
wondrous features, and highlight them in the ad. Ah yes,
that is the Teddy's face that launched a thousand ships!

Sell This Thing!

D o you and your child enjoy finding creative uses for oddball household items? If so, you'll find these activities fun and challenging—you dream up ideas for new gizmos and doofrabitizes. Your child draws or interprets the ideas, and then does a sales "demo" for the family. Who knows, you might even create a blockbuster product!

1. Whatchamacallit

What kind of machine could you make from several rectangles, a few ovals, some zig zags, bubbles, and assorted tree branches? We don't know either, but your child might have a good idea. Draw various shapes on the screen, and be sure to use the various options for the WACKY PENCIL and WACKY BRUSH. Explain to your child that you've drawn an unusual machine or appliance, and that his or her job is to "demo" it—stand by the computer, and try to sell you (or others in the family) on its outstanding abilities and qualities. Aha—that thing with the tree branches—maybe it's a necktie washer and egg beater?

2. Weird Tools

You probably won't find an earlobe stretcher or shoestring cleaner in your corner drug store. But you could have your child invent one with Kid Pix, and convince the family that they can't live without such things.

3. Quirky Combos

It's an alarm clock, a can opener, and a fly catcher—all in one. Try thinking up a strange combo gadget for your child to draw and sell to the rest of the family, perhaps the one product that will solve *everyone's* total hair care needs. And it's smaller than a credit card!

4. Group Design

How about if everyone in a group takes a turn adding to a drawing of a machine or gadget? The last person has the dubious honor of explaining what it does and then selling it to everyone else.

Logos and More

Look around your house, and you're bound to find dozens of product logos. You and your child can use Kid Pix to create your own product logos, as well as to design some spiffy packaging. Or perhaps your child could even create a "family logo," otherwise known as a coat of arms.

1. The Logo Design Shop

Some logos have a specific meaning, like RCA's dog listening to an old victrola. Others, like Mercedez Benz's circle divided into thirds, are more cryptic. Show your child several common items that have actual logos, then ask him or her to develop an original logo. Compare the results to the real thing, and see which your family likes better. Who knows—perhaps a famous maker of toothpaste really would pay a fortune for your child's logo calling for a great white shark with gaping jaws.

2. Wacky Product Packaging

Have your older child imagine that he or she has just been
hired as a designer by a company that makes an environ-
mentally correct snack food—it's so correct that even the
packaging, label, and yes, the logo, are edible!

3. Coat of Arms

In days of old, a family's coat of arms said a lot about
the family. Your child can make such a "logo" by using a
variety of Kid PiX tools, including the stamps. How about
an insignia that includes the following stamps: the busi-
nessperson, the clown, the hand with the pointed finger,
and the lightning bolt. This says, "We mean business—
except when we're clowning around."

Video Soapbox

D o your kids like to speak their minds on issues of the day—things going on in the household, school, and the world at large? If so, they'll love these activities—they provide an unprecedented excuse to spout off!

1. Extemporaneous Speeches

Here's an activity for turning your computer into a podium for unrehearsed speeches. One person draws something on the computer, and then another person (your child, for starters) gives a speech. The screen drawing might be something abstract—a rectangle for instance, which your child might decide symbolizes the school building. This might kick off a talk about the problems with education. Likewise, a drawing of an animal would be a great way to launch into a speech about endangered species. A picture of a trash can might lead to a talk about recycling, and a landscape with brown skies might generate some tough talk about air pollution.

By the way, if anyone is stuck on what to say about a square, how about talking about our favorite topic—television!

2. Strange Connections

In this activity, the "drawer" places two or more unrelated images on the screen, and the speaker must somehow tie them together. What would you or your child have to say about an oval, a stamp of a bicycle, and a stamp of a pirate's hat? Maybe the high cost of fixing flat tires these days!

3. My Favorite Things

One person says, my favorite thing in the whole wide world is. . . . And another draws a picture or places a stamp on the screen. The speaker then has to explain why whatever is pictured really is his or her favorite thing. What will you say when you find out yours is the stop sign or fried egg?

4. Reminiscences We Never Had

This activity is the same as the preceding, except the speaker says, "This reminds of the time. . . ." Watch out for this one—anything is possible!

Funny Money

Wouldn't it be nice to have your own mint? The kind that prints money, that is. Well, Kid Pix is the next best thing. While you won't be able to use your currency creations for tender, you and your child can have a million dollars worth of laughs.

1. Wild Bills

Most of our money is too serious-looking (although the old Pyramid with the Eye on our singles is pretty surreal). Why not lighten it up with a little Kid Pix Stamp Art? Draw a rectangle for the bill outline, then have your child choose an appropriate stamp. We like the ant on our four dollar bills, and the band aid on our six spots. Have your child draw other elements—people, buildings, animals, or mountain scenes, or add stamps to create interesting tender. Finally, choose a color to fill in the white space. Your money doesn't have to be green; "bluebacks" has a pretty nice ring, doesn't it?

2. Crazy Coinage

What ever happened to the buffalo nickel or the mercury dime? Your child can revive the imaginative tradition of

early engravers, and create money that's fun to look at.
Don't just think in terms of circles—who says coins have to
be round (other than the makers of pay phones, parking
meters, and vending machines)? Have your child experiment with interesting shapes, and use the stamp collection,
stamp editor, and freeform drawing tools to make coins
with pizazz—like the Stegosaurus thirty-seven cent piece or
the "complete non-cents piece."

3. Off the Wall Exchange Rates

Establish two currency "systems," then create bills and
coinage for both systems on opposite sides of the screen.
Decide on an exchange rate (round off to whole numbers),
then have your child use the MOVING VAN to convert one
system into the other, and vice versa. Yes, one Silver
Meatball is indeed worth four Blue Frosted Fish Cakes.

Now the Weather

One thing you can certainly say about today's television weather forecasts is that they're colorful. So colorful, in fact, that they were probably created with Kid Pix. Try these out on your junior weather forecaster, and learn about some pretty unusual meteorological conditions in your neck of the woods.

1. Batten Down the Hatches

Imagine your child appearing on the late night news to present the weather. He or she turns to the computer screen and says, "And according to our computer weather map. . . ."

Help out by drawing a map—real or imaginary—if your child can't make one by him- or herself. (Save the map for tomorrow night's show as well.) Your weathercaster will wan to create, among other meteorological images, clouds using the WACKY BRUSH, the LOOPER option. Another way to draw clouds is to erase them out of a solid background.

The ELECTRIC MIXER, SNOWFLAKES AND RAINDROPS option will also be invaluable. Hold the Option key (Mac) and the Ctrl key (PC) to create raindrops. Note that the SNOWFLAKES AND RAINDROPS option unpredictably spreads the drops and flakes all over the screen. So before you draw the map, your child might want to collect them on a blank screen with the MOVING VAN, and place them in the corner, and then later move them en masse to the desired portion of the map.

To spice up the map, encourage your child to add stamps. In addition to the obvious ones—the umbrella and the lightning bolt, why not use cats, dogs, and ducks to indicate a coming deluge, and a penguin for the big chill? And for those scorchers—nothing says it better than the fried egg!

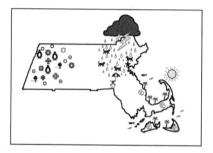

2. Weird Weather

In one of our favorite books, *Cloudy with a Chance of Meatballs*, by Judi and Ron Barrett, the residents of Chewandswallow eat all their meals from food that falls from the sky—until the weather takes a turn for the worse and everyone has to evacuate. Have your child make up a weird weather story of his or her own, using the stamps. Perhaps listeners to your child's forecast should be on the alert for heavy frog rains and musical winds, followed by a gradual clearing of turtles.

3. Weather from Another Planet

What's the weather forecast for Saturn, Pluto, or Alpha Centauri? Tune into Kid Pix weather, and find out for yourself!

Summer Vacation

R emember your first assignment each school year? It was probably to write a story about your summer vacation. Here's a way to use Kid Pix to turn this age-old yawner into a "mind bender" sure to delight the whole family.

1. High Adventure

Remember those lava flows your family barely escaped? The quicksand pit that almost ate the camper? And the King Cobra that hid in the food pack? Well, maybe not. But your child will. Have him or her illustrate your family's close calls and great escapes, then tell a story about each one. Suggest using Kid Pix tools to create drama. For instance, use the PAINT BUCKET to darken the sky from light and sunny to ominous and black, a volcano into a raging inferno, or a white-eyed crocodile into a red-eyed people-eater! When you crawl out from under your seat, you can take a turn at being the artist, too.

2. Time Travelers

Suggest that your family take a time vacation. Your child can illustrate the way, drawing dinosaurs (or using the stamps), knights, kings and queens, and the like. When it's your turn, you can explain how you got the brontosaurus egg through customs.

3. Sea World

No, this isn't about jumping dolphins and killer whales (although it could be). This is about the submarine voyage you took and the remarkable creatures of the deep you met along the way—like the angler fish with the light bulb on its head. Your child will fill in the details or perhaps even draw an octopus's garden in the shade.

4. Planetary Pleasures

Did you say that your last vacation was out-of-this-world? Have your child illustrate and describe your summer trip to Mars and beyond. Many of the inhabitants you met are probably right there in the stamp pad palettes. And the experience of space travel can be well simulated by many of the ELECTRIC MIXER tools. When your child is finished, beam down to the keyboard, and give your own rendition.

World Wonders

If the designers of the sphinx had Kid Pix, they probably could have built the great monument in half the time. And it would have had flashier colors, too. Well, the sphinx market is sewn up, but you and your child can still use Kid Pix to illustrate other wonders of the world, and to draw natural wonders that haven't even been discovered yet.

1. Amazing Towers

The Eiffel Tower. The Empire State Building. The Seattle Space Needle. These architectural feats pale by comparison to those that your child can create with Kid Pix. How about the Canine Palace, so named because it is fashioned out of giant dog bones? Or the Great Earth-Moon Foot Suspension Bridge? What's your child's wildest idea?

2. Natural Wonders

Old Faithful is an awesome sight. But your child can probably enlighten the world about all kinds of magnificent natural wonders that only he or she has discovered. Like the famous undersea fire pits in the Marianas Trench. Or the Mother of All Waterfalls in the Mohave Desert!

3. Fruity Cities

Imagine a modern city built inside a huge apple—the real "Big Apple." Or a whole city in which the buildings themselves were shaped like great pieces of fruit—the Big Fruit

Basket, with the Sigfried Kumquat Center being a monument to the town's first mayor.

4. Great Vegetable Wonders of the World

If it weren't for your child's authentic Kid Pix drawing of the 85-foot zucchini that had to be hauled around by a flatbed truck, no one would believe such a monster vegetable existed. What other astounding vegetarian wonders can your child illustrate?

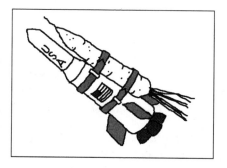

5. Extraordinary Creatures

No one knows what's become of the Loch Ness Monster, but your child can use Kid Pix to illustrate other legendary creatures—perhaps some that have been spotted in your own backyard, such as the Giant Winged Olive and the Great Glowing Ant!

Night Skies

F or urban dwellers, it's often hard to pick out constellations—city lights and tall buildings make it hard to distinguish stars that the ancients saw so clearly. So why not view your own constellations, right on your computer screen?

1. Do-It-Yourself Constellation

First, you'll need a clear and starry night (on your screen). Use the PAINT CAN to create a solid dark background on the drawing screen—that's your night sky. Next, you'll need some stars. Switch to the WACKY BRUSH, and select white from the color palette. From the tool options, choose A GALAXY OF STARS. The brush will leave a trail of stars as you move it around the screen with the mouse button pressed. Note: Move the mouse *quickly* to get a random display of stars; otherwise, your sky will be "clogged" with stars.

Now have your child look for patterns or objects among the stars. He or she can use the WACKY PENCIL with a thin line to connect the stars and create constellations. If your children can identify some "real" constellations, that's fine (might be worth a trip to the library for a star-gazer's book). But in any case, encourage creativity. What's wrong with Ursa Hare, the Winged Hamburger, or Zucchini Major?

2. Star Games

Whereas the preceding activity can be done by one person, this activity is designed for two or more people or teams. One person uses the WACKY BRUSH to place ten to twenty stars on the screen. Each time he or she presses and releases the mouse button, a star appears on the screen. The others must then identify a constellation that uses all the stars, and trace its outline with the WACKY PENCIL. (Imagine if *everyone* saw the Great Barbecue Tongs at the same time!)

3. "Reverse" Constellation-Making

Use the WACKY PENCIL (thin line, light color) to draw a picture on a white background. Place black stars along the outline (see Star Games), then fill the background with the PAINT CAN using the *same* color as the pencil line. This will wash out the lines, leaving only the stars. Ask your child to try using the WACKY PENCIL to connect the stars and recreate the drawing. The more stars, the easier it is to guess the picture—adjust the number for your child's age and abilities. OK, this *is* fudging it. But then again, the ancients didn't have Kid Pix.

Dreamscapes

D reams are the stuff of great art, and as these activities show, they lend themselves to the whimsical tools included with your Kid Pix program. Here are several ways your child can use his or her dreams as the subject matter for Kid Pix painting sessions. As a fringe benefit, you'll get a rare glimpse into the inner workings of your child's mind.

1. Dream Machine

Children and grownups alike can often remember only portions of their dreams. Why not use Kid Pix tools to pick up where the fun (or fear) left off? Encourage your child to illustrate a recent dream (morning folk might want to do this activity soon after their children wake up, while the dream is still fresh). Your child might want to use the dream as a story line, and create a new beginning or ending. This is also a great way to take the punch out of nightmares—after all, a monster that turns purple, and then gets erased or blown up by the FIRECRACKER, isn't much of monster, right?

2. The Protectors

This activity may provide some nightmare prevention for your child. It's adapted from a technique that we used to help our son, Noah, during a fearful period. We perched Noah's most valiant knights and ferocious dinosaurs on a shelf above his bed to guard him against anything that might invade his room. We're ready for the next round with a set of "dream protectors" that we created on Kid Pix.

To make your own protectors, first ask your child about the kind of qualities that a good dream guardian might have—powerful jaws, a great sword, a spiked tail, whatever. Let your child do the drawing. Print out the protectors, and then affix the drawings by your child's bed. Pleasant dreams!

3. Mixed Up Dreams

Freud said that dreams are the "Royal Road to the Unconscious." That might be true, but they're also the royal road to great stories. Give your child the elements (people, places, and events) of a dream you've recently had (editing the details, of course), and ask him or her to combine them in a picture story. Perhaps you'll finally figure out the significance of the intergalactic bath mat that's been visiting your sleep every night!

Cosmic Messages

Remember the old Chinese saying, a picture is worth a thousand words? Here's a set of activities that will allow you and your child to prove it—in most unusual ways.

1. Take Me to Your Leader

When NASA launched the two Voyager probes in 1977, it adorned both interplanetary craft with a metal plaque that would enable anyone (or anything) out there to understand a bit about us. The plaques depicted a man and a woman, our solar system, and chemical data about hydrogen.

Imagine that NASA is about to launch a new deep space probe and has hired your child to design a plaque for communicating with extraterrestrials. What kind of images would he or she include? Suggest the following images: a space map indicating the location of Earth (show other planets, stars, etc. for reference); Earth's climate and terrain; people and animals; and so on. Or how about an unmistakable landmark, like "Our House," with an arrow pointing to somewhere in the Western Hemisphere?

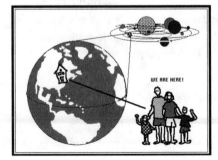

2. The Way We Were

Alright, the spacecraft bearing your child's message has left the Earth. In a few thousand years, we might hear back from ET or one of his cronies. In the meantime, you and your child might want to leave a message in a time capsule for future generations of (Earthling) anthropologists. Encourage your child to provide drawings and words that quickly communicate the important facts of the day, such as: his or her favorite foods and toys; current fashions; lyrics to pop songs; "in" colors; and great books.

Be sure your child writes the day and year—there's nothing more frustrating than finding a time capsule message with no date!

3. Message in a Bottle

Here's another activity that challenges your child's ability to create concise visual messages. Imagine that your family is stranded on a desert island with nothing but a computer and a proverbial glass bottle. You have a storage battery with enough juice to create one Kid Pix drawing. Have your child create a map that explains how you can be found. Then, sit back and soak in the rays while you're waiting to be rescued.

CHAPTER 4...

Video Olympics

Amazing Mazes

We've all played maze games at one time or another. They're fun and help develop your child's problem-solving abilities. Here's how to use Kid Pix to create some electronic versions that add a new dimension to the time-honored tradition of making mazes.

1. Mazeology 101

To create a maze, first use the PAINT CAN to fill the background with a color, black, or a dense dot pattern. Then, use the WACKY PENCIL with the widest round tip and white paint to mark a starting and finishing point. Use the TEXT tool to label them "Start" and "Finish." Draw a path between the two points, using the largest square tip. Make sure to include many right angle bends as well as switchbacks so that the path heads back to the start once or twice before reaching the end point. Now, wherever the path makes a right angle, add a branch that would allow the maze explorer to continue straight into an eventual dead end. (This makes the maze trickier to follow, since there's a natural tendency to go straight rather than take a turn.)

Save the maze, then have your child select the WACKY PENCIL with a fine line option, and see how he or she navigates through to the end. For younger children, keep the path simple; older kids will be challenged by a tortuous maze that fills the entire screen with mostly dead end pathways.

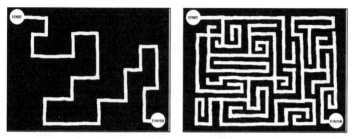

Step 1   Step 2

2. Hidden Endings

Construct a maze as in the first activity, but don't define
an end point. Instead, create numerous dead ends that
terminate in a circular area. Each area should contain a
hidden message (see *Secret Messages I and II*, pages 34
and 36) or a code (see *Code Busters*, page 22). One message or code should say, "Finish" or "You Did It." Others
might say "Quicksand Pit" or "Lion's Den," in which case
you start over.

Maze Explorers

I f your child enjoyed traversing through the pathways in
Amazing Mazes (page 80), he or she will definitely
appreciate the following activities, which turn maze
traveling into a high challenge!

1. Tricky Tools

It's one thing to follow the course of a maze with a straight
line, but another to do it with a tool like the WACKY BRUSH
that keeps changing form on you. The LEAKY PEN and
ZIG ZAG options make for especially interesting maze
exploration.

The LEAKY PEN produces a medium-sized line—as long as
you're moving. But if you stop to make a decision about
which way to go, the ink starts oozing. If that happens, use
the UNDO GUY, which will clean up the line back to the
beginning. Which is where the player goes to start over
again. For the ultimate challenge, have your child use the
ZIG ZAG option; as long as the mouse is flying, the line will
be fairly straight. But slow down at all, and the line will
take on a mind of its own!

2. Speedy Explorers

You can add a new level of excitement to the basic maze activity by introducing the element of time. See if your child can make it from start to finish without touching the sides of the walls—select a different color or screen so you'll see where he or she went off the beaten path.

3. High Stakes Maze Games

With this activity, the goal is to navigate the maze, and incur as few points as possible. Before letting anyone try the maze, agree on a pencil width or tool option, then agree on a scoring system. For instance, the traveler might receive one point every time his or her pencil line touches the walls (a real liability with the WACKY BRUSH, LEAKY PEN option). Taking a dead end might cost the traveler two points; after taking five dead ends, each one might cost ten points. Hope you have a steady hand when it's your turn!

Kid Cuts

D o your kids have an interest in cutting their own or their sibling's hair? Here's a way to channel that energy into something that's safe and has no chance of creating unintentional Mohawks (or intentional "rooster cuts")!

1. Makeover Artists

For this activity, you and your child draw a face, then add a full head of hair using the WACKY BRUSH and various options. Use the BUBBLY option for curly hair, NORTHERN LIGHTS for straight hair, and PINE NEEDLES for unkempt hair (the Option key, Mac, or Ctrl key, PC, creates a fried mozzarella cheese look). Then, of course, there's SPLATTER PAINT, ideal for high punk.

Now, move down, and give the face some eyebrows. Try all of the above options as well as a few of your own. Use PINE NEEDLES for a moustache. SPRAYPAINT makes for a great five o'clock shadow, while SWIRL creates a magnificent beard.

Once the face is done, your child can set about doing the makeover, using the various erasing tools to trim, shave, and shape. And for that punker, there's always the color palette, just in case he or she decides to go for a job interview.

2. Sheep Shearers

As a sideline to his or her hair-cutting business, your child might want to shear an even woollier creature. Draw a sheep as best you can; just about anything with four legs will look like a sheep when you cover its back, legs, head, and stubby tail with paint from the WACKY BRUSH, BUBBLY option. Choose a separate color for the fur, perhaps gray, so your child can see what he or she needs to erase. Then, arm your child with the "electronic" shears and—of course, three bags to fill!

Before   *After*

3. Tree Pruners

If your child tires of cutting hair for critters as wiggly as people and sheep, how about finding patrons who don't mind standing still? Use the TREES option of the WACKY BRUSH to generate a small orchard. Then, have your child trim any drooping or dead branches. And if he or she accidentally cuts down your favorite cherry tree, only one thing to do: Go to the stamp palette, and plant another one!

Obstacle Course

These activities are similar to the Amazing Maze games. But instead of presenting your child with decisions about which way to turn, they challenge your child by presenting lots of roadblocks.

1. Obstacle Course Builders

Fill the background with the PAINT CAN, then designate a starting point with the WACKY PENCIL and white paint. Use the broadest square-tipped option to draw a wiggly, zig zagging path that cuts through the background. Then create circular areas ("dot traps") along the path by using the largest round edge point. Fill in the circular areas with each of the screens chosen from the option palettes. You can choose screens from the option palettes of the OVAL, WACKY PENCIL, and WACKY BRUSH tools. When you've finished filling in a circular area, point the WACKY BRUSH in the middle, and select the MAGNIFYING GLASS option. This will enlarge the dots with each click—make the dots just large to accommodate the passage of a WACKY PENCIL line. Save your drawing.

The obstacle course is now ready. Your child uses the WACKY PENCIL in a color or shade of gray different from the rest of the course. On the monochrome system, try making the background black, and the course that the WACKY PENCIL uses to traverse it in white. Whatever kind of monitor you're using, the goal is for your child and other players to get through the course without going beyond the walls or touching any of the "obstacles" in it.

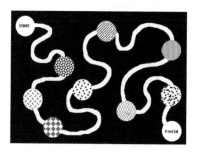

2. Hotshot Courses

Once your child becomes skilled at traveling through the course, suggest using wider WACKY PENCIL tips or the LEAKY PEN option of the WACKY BRUSH. And make it a rule that whenever a player hits the wall or an obstacle, he or she starts again.

3. Team Play

This obstacle course activity works like a relay race and is designed for a group of players. When the first player travels through one of the circular areas, he or she passes the baton (the mouse) to the next person in the group. Two people can play by alternating at every other "dot trap." Look sharp—your teammates are counting on you!

Kid Pix Sports

Believe it or not, you can use Kid Pix to play various "sports" games—two are described below. They won't build your muscles, but they'll certainly give you and your child a good chuckle (which is probably just as important).

1. Kid Pix Dart Game

No danger of poking holes in your computer here. Create three solid concentric circles by using the OVAL tool and the Shift key. It takes some practice to get the "nesting" right. Start with the outermost circle; otherwise you'll cover up the inner circles as you progress. Make each circle a distinctly different shade or color, and assign a point value. Save the file.

Now take turns throwing "darts" at the target. This is done by selecting the SPLASH option of the ELECTRIC MIXER. Whenever you or your child presses the mouse button, Kid Pix will generate a circle of color on the screen— but you never know where. After a certain number of "throws," tally up the points, and call up the original file to play another round.

Before

After

2. Fantasy Tennis

First, draw a tennis court as shown in the illustration. Choose stamps to represent players A and B. Position player A in the serving position and player B in the opposite court. The server then clicks on the ROLL-THE-DICE option of the WACKY BRUSH. Rolling a "1" means a good long hit; "2" means a shorter good hit; "3" represents a good hit to the left side of the court; "4" means a good hit to the right side; "5" is out of bounds, and "6" represents a serve that doesn't make it over the net. If the server "rolls" a "1," "2," or "3," he or she gets to move to either side of the court to wait for the return shot. A "4," "5," or "6" puts the serve in the other person's hands.

Player B now rolls the die. If he or she gets a "5" or a "6," Player A gets the point; with a roll of the die that sends Player B's shot to the opposite side of the court from where player A chose to stand, Player A automatically misses the shot and loses the serve. If player B rolls one of the other three over-the-net hits, then play continues and Player B gets to select a new position and Player A gets to roll the die. Score as you would with real tennis (fifteen, thirty, forty, love) for each set. Your computer screen today, Wimbledon tomorrow.

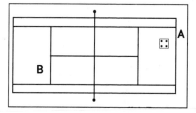

Stamp Olympics

Kid Pix stamps aren't just good for spicing up pictures and serving as tokens for board games; they lend themselves to a variety of activities involving manual dexterity and keen observation.

1. Rare Stamps

This game uses Kid Pix stamps to challenge your child's fine attention to detail. With your child looking the other way or in a different room, stamp out an image on the screen in the large or gargantuan size. Then, use the stamp editor (Goodies menu) to alter the stamp very slightly, perhaps only changing one pixel (dot of light), or perhaps inverting the colors or shading in one portion. Then, ask your child to point out the difference(s) in the modified stamp.

You can increase or decrease the difficulty by choosing simpler or more complex stamps and by using smaller stamp sizes. You can also modify several stamps, and place them among a screenful of unmodified stamps. Now *that* will be an interesting stamp collection!

What's the difference?

2. Where Have all the Strawberries Gone?

This activity will challenge your child's ability to manipulate fine detail on the screen. Select a stamp that has a lot of colors and components, such as the strawberry. Then, tell your child how you want the stamp modified with the stamp editor.

Let's say that you want to change the appearance of the strawberry—perhaps it should become less ripe. To "unripen" it, move the cursor to the pink color on your palette (if pink is available—you might have to change it to very overripe). Perhaps the strawberries are being enjoyed by caterpillars or worms. Darken a line of snaking pixels. How about this one—draw the strawberries that have been featured in this morning's bird buffet brunch!

3. Trace that Stamp

Select a stamp from one of the palettes and enlarge it to gargantuan size by pressing the Shift and Option keys (Mac) or Shift and Ctrl keys (PC) while you stamp a picture on the screen.

Then, using the WACKY PENCIL with the finest line, and in a different color than the stamp, try to trace the stamp as closely as possible without touching it. Finally, erase the stamp, and have your child add features to the outline, and color it. Perhaps even integrate it into a small scene, and draw a rectangle around it, which will give you the most common stamp of all: the postage stamp!

Steady Hand

Imagine balancing a glass of water on the tips of your fingers as you hop around an obstacle course. Well, you and your child can have almost the same thrill with these activities. And if you flub it, you'll stay dry!

1. Precision Line Drawing

Can your child draw a vertical line without deviating to the left or right? Find out with this activity. Select the WACKY PENCIL, and choose the option for the least dense dot screen. Have your child place the cursor at the top, and then draw slowly to the bottom. In order for the dots to show up on the screen, your child will have to keep the line perfectly vertical. Any shift to the left or right, and the line breaks or disappears. How steady is your hand?

2. Precision Erasing

This one's a lot harder than it looks. Draw a line, then have your child erase it with the tiniest eraser option. The idea is to follow the course of the line. The more treacherous and twisting the line, the harder the exercise. When your child's done, have him or her draw a line for you to erase. Take a deep breath. Center yourself. Go for the gold!

3. Brickyard

Create a stack of "bricks" in one corner of the screen. This is done by drawing a small rectangle and filling it with an appropriate color (blue bricks are OK). Then use the Option key (Mac) or the Ctrl key (PC) with the MOVING VAN tool to clone the brick. Keep doing this until you have a good pile of them. Make some half-sized bricks, too. Save the file. Now have your child use the MOVING VAN tool to transport the bricks one by one, and align them so they make a wall with "mortar joints." The half-bricks are used to fill in the ends, and create a perfect wall. This calls for precision work, especially if your child uses the MAGNET option to move the pieces. Finally, why not allow your child to use the WACKY PENCIL for a little writing on the wall—you can always wash away the graffiti with a click of the UNDO GUY!

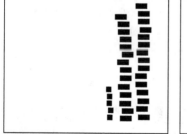

Before

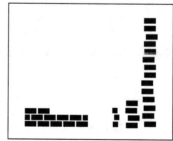

After

Two Right Hands

Skip this collection of activities if you're ambidextrous. But if you're like most of us, you'll find the following activities both fun and challenging. You'll also gain true appreciation for what the other hand can and cannot easily do.

1. Kid Pix Navigation

In this exercise, you and your child try to use the mouse with your nondominant hand. (Your child will probably have an easier time of it.) Make sure that the list of things to do includes selecting menu items, colors, tools, and options. Note what's easy and what's difficult—and compare notes with your child.

2. Agility Builders

Have your child use his or her nondominant hand to maneuver through mazes (see pages 80 and 82, and obstacle courses, page 86). You might also suggest trying the *Steady Hand* activities on page 92.

3. Copy Cats

Here's a real test of ambidexterity. Make a drawing using the fine line of the WACKY PENCIL with your dominant hand. Then, try making the same drawing (duplicating or tracing it) with your other hand and a different color. How does it compare, and how do your attempts compare to your child's?

4. Switch Offs

In this activity, two people take turns drawing different parts of a suggested picture—using their nondominant hands to move the mouse. Try not to botch your child's drawing too badly!

5. Drawing with the Other Side of the Body

Once you and your child have gotten the hang of using the mouse with your nondominant hand, try this: Make a stack of rectangles, a line of ovals, and so on. Then, try making a face, a house, or an animal. How about a family portrait? Be ready with explanations—"No, Emily, I don't that your hair looks like you just stuck your finger in the electric socket" and "Yes, Dad, I think I did draw your nose a bit too large. . . ."

Speed Readers

I s the computer screen, like the hand, really quicker than the eye? Find out with these activities, which will give everyone's eyes and brains the utmost challenge.

1. Disappearing Images

For this activity, you'll need to create a few images on the screen—freeform drawings, geometrical shapes, a collection of stamps, and so on. This should be done with your child out of the room or facing away from the screen. When the arrangement is complete, save it, then select the ERASE tool and the FADE AWAY option, but do not trigger it yet—have your finger ready on the button. Ask your child to come study the screen, then trigger the ERASER tool. When the screen is cleared away, ask your child if he or she can remember what was on the screen, and where it was located. Compare it to the original—seeing is believing!

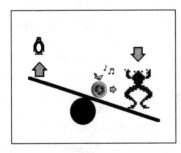 

For younger kids, keep it simple by using only a few shapes or stamps and selecting ERASER options that gradually clear away the screen. Older kids will find it great fun take on all the screen elements before, say, the SWEEP option vaporizes the images. In any case, experiment with all the ERASE options—they all have different time delays and work in different ways. If there's an option that you particularly like, but it works too slowly, then have your child view the screen a certain number of seconds after you've initiated it. Now, won't it be a blast if, when it's your turn, your child uses the FIRECRACKER option to clear the screen for you?

2. Vanishing Words

This activity is similar to *Disappearing Images*, except that it uses words instead of pictures. Younger children will enjoy reading their names or a few easy words before the screen clears. You can make the game quite complex for older kids by placing different parts of a sentence in differ-ent portions of the screen. You can also enter a passage from a book or a poem, and see how much your child can absorb before the screen clears.

Now You See It...

I f you enjoyed the *Speed Reading* activities on the preceding page, then try these. They'll challenge your child in different ways and offer additional opportunities for family Kid Pix fun.

1. Transforming Colors

Paint a few different color swatches or parallel lines of different colors on the screen. Your child should be facing the other direction while you do this. Save the file, then have the ELECTRIC MIXER, NIGHT AND DAY option ready to fire. Have your child look at the screen for a short time. Then, trigger the INVERTER, and the colors will instantly change. Can your child remember the original colors?

2. Speed Sorting

Choose three to four shapes, colors, stamps, and so on, and scatter them on the screen in varying quantities (four pink circles from the WACKY PENCIL, five heart stamps, and three tree stamps). Save the file.

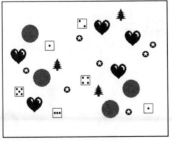

Before

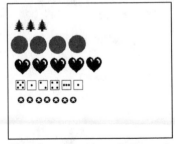

After

For younger children, ask them to manually sort the like objects with the MOVING VAN, then arrange the screen items from most to least. For older children, use the timed screen erasers so that they have to quickly assess and count the pictures on the screen before the erasers do their dirty work. When the dust settles, ask your child if he or she remembers how many of each shape or stamp were on the screen.

To increase the difficulty, you can place rectangles of dot screens over different portions of the screen—this will make it hard for your older child to determine what's what. As you can see, things can get complex very quickly!

Math Whizzes

These activities are similar to *Speed Readers*, but are designed to help children develop and enjoy using their mathematical skills.

1. Line 'Em Up

Use the LINE tool with the widest square tip to draw several parallel straight lines of the same length but in different colors. (You now have a set of "cuisenaire rods," a favorite math "manipulative" for teaching math to younger children.) You can use the MAGNET option of the MOVING VAN to trim off the right and left edges, so the lines are of uniform length. Use the MOVING VAN to randomly "chop" all of the rods, except one, into segments. For all but one of the segmented rods, erase one of the segments. Then, ask your child which of the rods, when reassembled, will equal the length of the unsegmented rod. Your child can manually reassemble the rod with the MOVING VAN, or try it mentally. For older kids, make the thrown away segments mere slivers—quite a challenge even for mathematical whiz kids!

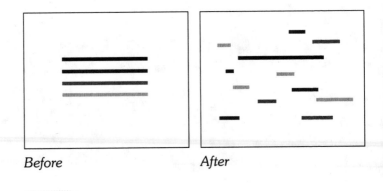

Before   *After*

2. Fast Computations (for Older Kids)

The mechanics for this activity are the same as in the first activity of Speed Readers. Instead of using images or words, however, the activity uses numbers and requires some mathematical manipulation. The goal is for the reader to remember all the numbers that were on the screen before they were erased, then sum them up. Alternatively, you might place a string of numbers on the screen with arithmetical operators from the third palette. (You'll have to use the letter *X* for multiplication.)

Or, don't provide the operators at all, but give an end result; your child must not only remember the string, but must also figure out how to use the numbers to arrive at the result you specify. That means you'll have to do a little planning of your own ahead of time so the numbers all work. If you're lucky, your child won't ask *you* to do any advanced calculus when it's your turn!

Moving Day

Moving has to be one of the more odious activities we can think of. But we all have to do it at one time or another. (The average American family moves seven times during its natural history.) Here are a few moving exercises that are not only painless but actually fun!

1. Cross Town

Create a multi-story house with the LINE and RECTANGLE tools, as shown in the illustration on the next page. Furnish it with common items (from the STAMP tool palettes). Then, draw a moving truck to the right of the house, and make it big enough to hold all of the items in the house when packed well. The goal of the activity is for your child to "carry" each object individually to the van (with the MOVING VAN tool, MAGNET option). He or she should try to pack the entire moving truck, remembering that objects must be unpacked later and moved individually to the "new" house. Explain that the movers shouldn't cram things so close that the MAGNET tool can't be used to separate them.

Once the truck is packed, use the ELECTRIC MIXER'S WRAP AROUND option to scroll the house to the far right. This will push the truck off the right side of the screen and onto the left—the cross town journey. Now have your child "drive" the truck (via the MOVING VAN tool) to the "new" house (you may want to change the roof color, etc.), then use the MAGNET option to unpack it. Hope nothing breaks!

Before   *After*

2. The Crate Pretenders

A variation on the *Cross Town* activity involves "crating up" all the furnishings in the house. In this activity, your child uses the RECTANGLE tool to draw a box around each stamp. He or she then moves the boxes out to the truck with the MAGNET option of the MOVING VAN tool. The real challenge comes when the mover tries to unpack the crates once they've been moved into the new house; that requires using the finest ERASER option to remove the crate around each item. It may be tricky, but at least it's ecological—there's no cardboard to throw out!

3. Mad Movers

For added fun, give your child a time limit for cleaning out the house and moving to the new one. See if he or she (or other players) can break a previous personal record—without "breaking" anything else (unintentionally erasing part of it)!

CHAPTER 5...

Screen Gems

....

Not Elephant

According to an ancient Chinese tale, a great Zen sculptor was once asked how he created his remarkable statues of elephants. The sculptor replied, "Simple. I just carve away everything that is not elephant." You and your child can continue this tradition right on your computer screen using Kid Pix ERASERS tools.

1. Eraser Painting

Kid Pix offers a marvelous array of erasing tools, from wholesale destruction (FIRECRACKER) to fine "chisel point" tools (the smallest ERASERS box options). You can also erase by selecting white from the color palette and using the WACKY PENCIL.

For this activity, soak the background with a solid color or pattern using the PAINT CAN, then give your child the task of creating a drawing by using only the ERASERS tools to clear away everything that is "not elephant." Specify what you would like him or her to draw. When your child finishes, it's your turn to paint (that's "erase," actually) a picture of his or her choosing.

With this activity, it's easy to adjust the level of challenge. Players can stipulate the type of ERASERS option that their fellow sculptors must use, as well as the content of the drawing. This is all trickier than it seems—at least for those of us not steeped in the Zen tradition.

2. Move-it Painting

This activity is similar to *Eraser Painting*. But instead of using erasers, the Kid Pix sculpture uses the MOVING VAN and its various options to move pieces of the solid background color. This will leave a white outline and a solid color interior to the "sculpture" piece. This is significantly more challenging, because it's much harder to create smooth edges with the rectangular tools.

3. Random Erasers

With the preceding activities, the artist had control over the erasing process. To add an element of unpredictability, use the WHITE CIRCLES option for the ERASERS. Each time you press the mouse button after selecting the option, several large white circles will randomly dissolve part of the background. Your child, or whoever is drawing, must then make something from whatever background is left—using other ERASERS tools to finish the sculpture.

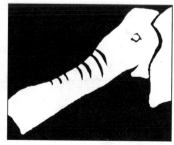

Before   *After*

Geometry Drawings

I t's one thing to draw a landscape, streetscape, or portrait with a full complement of drawing tools. But what if you were limited to certain regular geometrical shapes? Whisk yourself to the "Geo Zone," and find out for yourself!

1. Squares and Circles

In this activity, the idea is to create a world based on nothing but squares (created by holding the Shift key while using the RECTANGLE tool) and circles (do the same with the OVAL tool). The artist can use fill patterns and shading within the forms, too. Start off with a simple scene involving, say, a house and a tree, then up the ante by adding people and animals. Perhaps try a whole urban scene or landscape. Portraits can be a real challenge, too.

And for the ultimate test of skill? Use only the octagon tool. Oops, there isn't one! So your child will have to create each octagon—from scratch!

2. Connected Drawings

With this activity, the idea is to draw something using contiguous geometrical shapes. The artists can use any of the drawing tool shapes, or use the LINE tool to create triangles, pentagons, and so on. The only rule is that the shapes have to be regular and must be connected at some point. Call out the number of objects to be drawn, then see how your child makes the connections.

3. Copy Drawing

Create several geometrical objects on one side of the screen. Leave enough space between them so you can use the MOVING VAN to copy them. After placing the box around the object to be copied, hold down the Option key (Mac) or the Ctrl key (PC), and then press the mouse button. Drag the copy of the image to the desired location, and release the mouse button. Provide enough interesting shapes, and your child may recreate the Great Pyramid of Cheops by the end of the day!

Paint by Colors

All of us played with "paint-by-number" sets at some point during our childhoods. Why not extend that grand tradition to the computer age? Here are some variations on the paint-by-number theme that you can do with your Kid Pix program.

1. Do-It-Yourself Paint by Number

First, draw a figure with the WACKY PENCIL. Then, randomly subdivide the picture and the background into "watertight" compartments (that is, make sure none of the lines are broken. Otherwise, when you apply the PAINT CAN later in the process, the paint will "leak out"). Be sure to use the same kind of lines when you subdivide the drawing: Use rounded lines for rounded drawings and angular lines for angular drawings. Now, use the TEXT tool to place a number or letter in each compartment. You can place a correspondence key at the bottom of the screen, or see if your child can remember the color assignments. Save your file.

> Hint: Make sure that you indicate different colors for different portions of the background; if the background is one solid color, the outline of the drawing will become apparent, taking out the element of surprise for your child.

Explain the idea to your child, then turn over the PAINT CAN and watch as your masterpiece comes to life.

2. Paint by Color

This activity is similar to the preceding, except that instead of putting a number in each compartment, you use a small rounded tip of the WACKY PENCIL to apply a dot of the actual color you want your child to use.

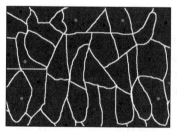

Before   *After*

3. Paint by Texture

Here's a "paint by" activity ideal for monochrome systems. It's also fascinating on a color system. The idea is to fill in the compartments with a dot screen pattern (black or one color). Use the OVAL tool to place a sample of the texture to be used in each compartment. Choose the patterns so that there is adequate contrast between the object and the background. The simplicity can lead to some delightfully pleasing results.

Great Masters

Even young children can appreciate the different styles of paintings in your local museum. Here's a way to introduce some traditional styles in your family room gallery.

1. The Realists

As the name suggests, the idea here is to have your child draw as accurate a rendition of real world objects as possible. If your computer is by a window, suggest that the Kid Pix artist look out and recreate the scene with as much detail as possible. Or, place a vase near the computer. Or, in the Andy Warhol tradition, a can of soup. Encourage your child to capture everything about the object he or she is drawing. Perhaps combine the elements, and join in yourself. Can't you picture yourself next to "Whistler's Mother"—"Mom with Can of Chicken Noodle, Dandelions, and Toaster?"

2. The Impressionists

Ah, those dreamy, flowing paintings of Monet! Use the WACKY PENCIL with a medium-sized rounded tip and the WASH option to create a lovely mosaic of gentle colors and shapes.

3. The Pointillism School

Georges Seurat may have wished dot-making was as simple as it is with Kid Pix, when he created his famous "A Sunday on the Grande Jatte." Use the PENCIL with the smallest

ROUND POINT option to paint by dots. Lots of them. It might take a whole Sunday, but the results will be stunning!

4. The Surrealists

Salvador Dali's dripping clocks may or may not be your idea of art. But one thing is certain: Kid Pix tools can generate some pretty surreal-looking images. Try using the WACKY BRUSH with the LEAKY PEN or FUZZER options.

5. The Jackson Pollack Splatter

Jackson Pollack isn't the only one who can toss paint on a canvas. Try using the WACKY BRUSH with the MAGNIFYING GLASS option and the WACKY PENCIL with the largest rounded tips. And when you sell your child's screen works, you might be able to spring for one of those 21-inch color monitors!

Bouquets Unlimited

Why wait for spring or an official horticultural event when your computer screen can be in full bloom all year round? Your child can use a variety of Kid Pix tools to create a magnificent bed of annuals.

1. Basic Bouquets

In addition to manually drawing petals with the WACKY PENCIL, your child will find a number of WACKY BRUSH options very useful when drawing flowers. Suggest that your child use the TREE option in green to draw a handful of stems. Then, to create petals, he or she can use the following WACKY BRUSH options: BUBBLY, LEAKY PEN, PINE NEEDLES, THE LOOPER, SWIRL, SPRAY PAINT, GEOMETRY, PIES, ECHOES, and CATERPILLARS. The possibilities are only limited by your and your child's "electronic green thumb."

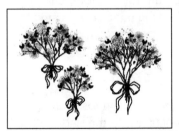

2. Wild Flower Delights

Have you ever driven in the country and admired fields of wild flowers? Your child can create a similar effect with many of the Kid Pix tool options. Start off with a screen or "field" of light green using the largest rounded point of the WACKY PENCIL with the WASH option. Then, add flowers using the smaller rounded points and the WACKY BRUSH options listed above. You might suggest the use of the MAGNIFYING GLASS option to enlarge certain varieties from your child's own Kid Pix horticultural laboratory.

3. Stamp It Out

Want some realistic drawings? Use the flower images on the stamp palettes. Your child can arrange them into corsages, headbands, and various other pieces of finery. Place enough flower stamps on the screen, and you might even begin to smell strange fragrances emanating from your computer.

4. Pick a Flower

Create a flower bed along the bottom of your screen, say, about an inch deep. Draw stems using the WACKY PENCIL and flowers using the tools described above. Make sure that none of the flowers are wider or taller than the tallest MOVING VAN rectangle. Then, use the RECTANGLE tool to draw a vase of a complementary color. Pluck a few flowers, move them to the vase using the MOVING VAN, and arrange the picked flowers. Enjoy your new centerpiece.

Molecular World

Of course, everything in this world is composed of atoms and molecules. But what if we could *see* the individual building blocks that make up people, trees, goldfish, and potato chips?

1. Atomic Drawing

No, you don't need a Ph.D. in physics to do this activity. And it's perfectly safe, too. The idea is to create a stockpile of basic "atomic" building blocks, and then use them to make complex drawings. Use the SHAPES AND MORE SHAPES option of the WACKY BRUSH to place various triangles, circles, and other forms in one corner of the screen. Erase duplicate shapes, and be sure to leave enough space around the shapes so that your child can copy them with the MOVING VAN—use the VAN to spread them apart, if necessary. To copy the atoms, your child places the MOVING VAN square around the selected shape, holds down the Option key on the Mac, or the Ctrl key on the PC, then presses the mouse button, and drags the clone of the image to the place on the screen where he or she wants it.

So what *does* the world look like at the atomic level? Scientists across the planet are waiting with baited breath!

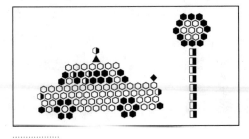

2. Molecular Drawing

This activity is similar to the preceding, except that instead of dealing with individual "atoms," you've moved up to the "molecular level." Connect several atoms (shapes) with straight lines to create a molecule. Leave enough space around the molecule to copy it with the MOVING VAN tool. The more variety in the molecules you create, the richer your drawings. And the greater the challenge of fitting everything together.

3. Building Codes

Try either of the preceding activities, but stipulate that the atoms or molecules must always be applied in a specific order; say, a circle must always be followed by two rectangles and a triangle, or a certain molecule must be repeated twice before using another one. It works in nature, so why not try it on your screen!

Stamp Art

Who says that you can only draw with "convention-al" tools—like the WACKY PENCIL or PAINT BRUSH? In fact, your child can "draw" with stamps by laying down a "bead" of images. While it takes a bit of practice to control the exact placement of the stamps, the results can be quite surprising, as you'll see in these activities.

1. Aiken Drum Stamp Face

Does your child know the folk song called "Aikendrum"? It's about a man named Aikendrum who lived in the moon. Among other unusual features, his body was made of watermelon and his hair of spaghetti. Take turns with your child using the STAMP tool to recreate old Aiken right on your computer screen. You can take a thematic ap-proach, using flowers, vehicles, animals and so on for features, or randomly choose different stamps to create a pair of eyes, a nose, and the like. When you're done, think up a song of your own, perhaps about a man who lived on Mars and. . . .

2. Stamp Landscapes

Choose stamps with the appropriate shapes and colors for your child to draw the outlines of hills, valleys, mountains, volcanoes, lakes, rivers, and the like. For example, use the brown chair for tree trunks and branches, or green frogs for the leaves. Your child can also place single enlarged stamps in the landscape, in which case a horse becomes a horse and not part of a drawing line.

3. Stamp Words

In addition to using stamps to draw the outlines and details of faces and landscapes, have your child try creating words from stamp images. Here, the choice of stamp themes can add an interesting dimension to the message. For instance, try writing, "Happy Valentine's Day" with hearts, "Take me to your leader" with human or animal footprints, or "Exit" with the pointing finger.

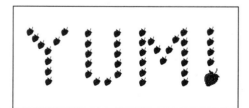

CHAPTER 6...

Electronic Bookworks

Group Drawing

I t might be the case that two mice can't occupy the same screen at the same time (second law of rodent dynamics). But two or more artists can certainly participate in the same drawing, proving that great art can indeed be produced by committee.

1. Chapter by Chapter

In this activity, one person gives an opening storyline, such as, "The great fish moved silently through the night water, propelled by short sweeps of its crescent tail." (No, we didn't make that one up—it's the opener of *Jaws*.) That person illustrates the idea and saves the file. The next person then adds a "chapter" (an illustration to the story in a new file), but doesn't verbally explain his or her idea for the continuing storyline. Continue until the last person has created a chapter in the electronic book.

When the last chapter is concluded, "play back" the story, opening each file and leaving it on-screen long enough for someone other than the artist who drew the scene to explain it. This will no doubt lead to some wild interpretations!

2. Tales for Two

This chain story activity is designed for two people. One person begins by drawing a picture to begin the story. The second person then tells the story based on the picture and contributes his or her own picture to continue the story that's been told so far. The first person then picks up the storyline and adds to it by drawing a new picture. This "volley" continues until the story reaches a happy or hilarious ending.

3. Telephone Chain Story

This activity is meant to be played with groups of Kid Pix artists. The first person makes up a short story and whispers it to the second person, who illustrates it, then saves and closes the file. The second person verbally passes the story on to a third, who also illustrates the tale and saves his or her work. After everyone has drawn the story, compare the files. Amazing how the dog became a hog, which became the log that ate the phone!

Vacation Book

Earlier in this book, you might have done one of the
zany activities called *My Summer Vacation*, which
involved illustrating whimsical journeys that happen
only in the imagination. Now it's time for the real thing.

1. Vacation Snapshots

Have your child draw pictures that record what your family
did on a memorable vacation. His or her pictures might
portray the family playing at a park, making a sand castle,
playing miniature golf, collecting seashells, fishing, or having a picnic. Or perhaps rubbing first aid cream onto
Mom's lobster-red back!

2. Vacationland

Does your child sometimes ask, "Where was it that we saw
the dog catch the frisbee last summer when we were on
vacation?" If so, help him or her draw a simple map showing the lay of "vacationland." It doesn't matter whether it's
accurate or not—the idea is to record your child's warm
memories of a vacation, and keep them fresh throughout
the year.

3. Souvenir Shop

Souvenirs aren't just for fun. They also help us remember a
vacation's high and low points, and moments of comic
relief. Draw an object related to the vacation, then ask your
child to talk about it in his or her own words. Type the

description by using the Option key (Mac) or the Ctrl key (PC) and the TEXT tool. Then, have your child select a "souvenir" for you to describe—you might be surprised to learn what your child thought was most memorable on your last trip!

4. Vacation Calendar

Yet another way to get children to remember the details of a vacation is to create a calendar, and describe each day away from home. Divide the screen into squares representing each day of your vacation. Use numbers or letters from the palettes of the TEXT tool to indicate the day, then have your child use stamps to designate your mode of transportation, the weather, the activities your family did, and any memorable events.

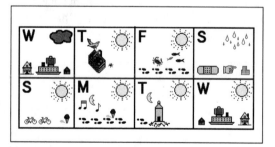

Kid Pix Funnies

Do your kids enjoy reading or looking at the comic strips in the newspaper? If so, they can use Kid Pix to create their own. Here are several activity suggestions for starting your Kid Pix Funnies Press.

1. Picture Cartoons

Have your child select several characters from the stamp palettes, and make up a short story about them. Help decide where the story can logically get broken. Then, use the RECTANGLE tool to draw a box extending the full width of the screen. You can also use the RECTANGLE tool to subdivide the box into as many compartments as you have story segments. Use the PAINT CAN to fill in the background of the compartments, as needed, then add the stamps (regular or enlarged size). Is it really that simple? Sure, just look at the comic strip below. Scene 1: Dog chases cat. Scene 2: Dog closes in on cat. Scene 3: Big cat comes on the scene. Scene 4: Big cat chases dog up tree!

2. Chain Cartoon

In this activity, you and your child take turns using stamps to create a comic strip. As in the previous activity, draw a rectangle with compartments, then study the stamp palettes until you "see" a story in the pictures, such as a helicopter meeting a flying saucer. Print the two images in the first compartment, along with several building and tree stamps to give a sense of height. Your child, or another family member, should continue the story line and might choose to have the helicopter follow the flying saucer into star-studded outer space. You might give the story an unexpected twist with an intergalactic stoplight floating in space. Your child might then decide to outdo you, and show both vehicles waiting for the light while a skateboarder crosses in front.

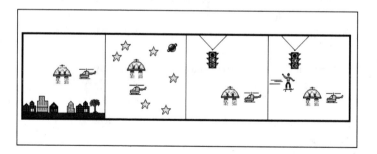

Story Illustrators

P arents and teachers spend a lot of time reading books and telling stories to kids. Here's how children can get involved with stories in a way that the whole family can enjoy—through original illustrations.

1. Junior Book Illustrators

Do you have a favorite story that you tell your child? Why not have your child illustrate it with Kid Pix. Discuss with your child the parts of the story that he or she likes best, then talk about what might go into pictures tailored to the plot. This is a great opportunity to use Kid Pix stamps in addition to the drawing tools. Also, encourage your child to use different colored backgrounds and fills with the PAINT CAN.

As you read or tell the story, your child can call up the appropriate files (you might have to help younger kids). Hint: Name each drawing with a sequential file number, so that you can easily retrieve it at the right time (for example, MOUSEKIN1, MOUSEKIN2, etc.). By the way, if you have a computer capable of recording sound (see Introduction), this is a great opportunity to embed a storyline or message such as, "Turn the page, please." (Refer to the Kid's Pix Crash Course for details.)

2. Tell Me a Story

Does your child like to tell tall tales (other than how the cookie jar emptied itself)? You can draw on that ability by having him or her illustrate an original story, then present it to you or to friends. As in the previous activity, help your child name the files sequentially, such as TIGER1, TIGER2, and so on, so that the story moves along frame by frame.

For younger children, a single picture file may be sufficient to capture the entire story; it's remarkable how much information a five-year-old can pack into a single piece of art! (Besides, brevity is an art form in itself. As the philosopher and mathematician Blaise Pascal wrote, "I have made this letter longer than usual, because I lack the time to make it short.")

Shuffle Book

T he shuffle book really isn't a book at all—it's a collection of cards with images on them. You shuffle the cards around, and presto, you have new story. The computer is ideal for creating shuffle books; all you have to do is save each page as a separate file, then call up the pages in any order you wish.

1. The Visual Shuffle Book

The simplest type of shuffle book contains pictures that members of the family have drawn. Each picture, which resides in a separate file, should have distinctive elements. For example, one file might have a picture of a cow eating grass, another of an airplane, and another of a house. You would then retrieve the files, one at a time, and each person would interpret the pictures. The story so far might go something like, "While mother cow stood placidly eating grass, an airline flying overhead scared the daylights out of her and sent her running for cover into the farmer's house, where she hid under the bed."

If your computer can record sounds when running Kid Pix (see Introduction), you can attach voices or music to each shuffle book page file. The sounds might be authentic cow impersonations, music to chew your cud by, jet airplane engines, or, more mundanely, a note about which file to open next.

2. Text Shuffle Book

Whereas the visual shuffle story leaves the plot completely up for interpretation, you can guide the story along with selected text. For example, using the cow, airplane, and house, the text accompanying the picture of a cow might say something like: "The prized Holstein had just finished her dinner." The airplane text might read, "Far above the ground, the flight attendants in the jumbo jet were getting ready to serve lunch." And for the house, the text could say, "No one had been home for three days." As each page appears on the screen, the storytellers must somehow use the exact phrase in the story. As you can see, it requires a lot of creativity to make a coherent story. But the results, as you'll find, can be hilarious!

3. Mini-Shuffle Story

Use the RECTANGLE tool to make six separate boxes to fill the screen. Then, create six small scenes with the STAMP tool, numbering them from one to six with the TEXT tool. Use the die from ROLL-THE-DICE (WACKY BRUSH) to determine which picture you or your child must weave the story around next.

Stamp Stories

Each Kid Pix stamp is a story waiting to be told by children (and grownups) of all ages. This activity set provides a number of ways in which you and your family can use the stamp collections to inspire great tales that will excite the imagination of all who listen.

1. Story Machine

In this activity, one person serves as the "stamper," pumping out a variety of stamps to keep the storyline going. Other players can take turns creating stories as a new stamp image appears on the screen. It's up to the stamper how long the storytellers must talk about each image. OK, enough—fifteen minutes on the tea cup is too much!

2. Priceless Words

Even preschoolers can enjoy reading a story if consists mainly of pictures, such as the Kid Pix stamps. Tell the story with stamps (create your own with the Edit Stamp function, if you wish). Fill in the plot with just a few connecting words, using the TEXT tool with the Option key (Mac) or the Ctrl key (PC). Maybe the pictures won't be worth a thousand words, but they'll be priceless nonetheless!

3. Stamp Story Title

Want to spice up your stamp story? Create a stamp "puzzler title." A puzzler title uses stamps and the plus and minus signs to modify the name of the picture. For example, "S + [MOON STAMP] - M" would yield the word "Soon" (substitute S for the M in "Moon"). Can you or your child figure out the popular story title in the puzzler shown below?

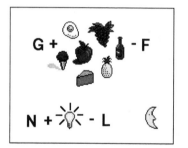

4. Surprise Stamp Story

Use the TEXT tool with the Option key (Mac) or Ctrl key (PC) to type out a simple story rich in simple nouns. Delete the nouns and leave enough space for a stamp where the nouns would have appeared. Read the story back to yourself, and whenever you encounter a "hole," ask your child to select a stamp for it. You can suggest a classification for the stamp—animal, place, food, vehicle, household object, and so on, or you can let him or her randomly choose. When all the blanks are filled in, read the story. If your child has selected stamps randomly, you'll probably be in store for some belly laughs!

CHAPTER 7...

Kid Pix
Printouts

....

Family Gazette

Every family can use its own gazette—gazettes are fun to design and make it easy to keep in touch with friends during holidays. Here are some suggestions for breaking into household publishing and capturing all the home-front news that's fit to print.

1. That's News!

First things first. Create a "masthead" for your family gazette using the TEXT tool. Be sure to add a distinctive logo from the stamp palettes. Save the file. Each time you add text, save it under a new name so you keep your master "template" clean. And what should you write about? Upcoming family outings. Reviews of the latest read-aloud book. School news. And the results of family surveys and "Gallup Polls" about pressing issues such as preferred ice cream flavors and Dad's new haircut.

2. "Z" is for Zodiac

What do the stars have in store for your family members? They'll know when you add another section—the family horoscope, complete with its own symbols (stamps) and prognostications. Good news! If you were born under the sign of the table, you're going to have a great day!

3. Sunshine, Clouds, and Rain

Should family members take their umbrellas today? Definitely. The weather report in the early morning edition of your gazette predicts clear skies for your backyard—but torrential rains are likely from your front door to the bus stop. Good luck!

4. Super Sunday

Do you have any sports aficionados in your family? Good. Put them to work as reporters for your gazette's sports section. Report on school and family games, and upcoming sports events. Pass the Kid Pix, and play ball.

5. Lonely Hearts

Once you've mastered the basic news beat, add a personal advice column with real family issues or just zany questions. Call it something like "Ask Dad," and take turns asking questions and responding as "Dad." When you're done, your family shouldn't have a care left in the world!

Game Boards

H ere are several game boards that are easy to make and fun to use. And they won't cost you anything more than the paper they're printed on. Good cheap fun at its best!

1. Hits and Misses

To play this game for two, create a ten squares by ten squares grid using the LINE tool. Place the letters A through J across the top with the STAMP tool, and the numbers one through ten down the left side. Save your file, then print out two grids for each player. On one grid, each player outlines groups of squares. These are the targets. Decide ahead of time the number of targets and how many squares the targets must each occupy in total. Take turns calling out a coordinate, such as "F3." If that lands in one of the other person's targets, he or she calls out "hit." The first person records the results on his or her blank grid. The second person then calls out a coordinate, and the game continues until each person has hit or identified the location of all the targets.

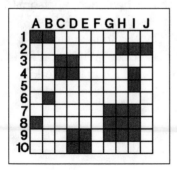

2. Dot the Box

Here's a great game for passing the time on long trips, long restaurant waits, long doctor's office waits, or just about anytime. Create a solid background with the PAINT CAN, then use the widest LINE tool with white paint. Cover the screen with vertical lines, each separated by a tiny space. Do the same with horizontal lines. You will now have a series of perfectly spaced dots (or tiny squares). Save the file for future printouts or on-screen use. Now for the game. Players take turns connecting two dots with a line. Wherever the lines create three sides of a box, you can put a "lid" on it, initial the box, and keep doing so as long as there are three-sided boxes left. When the board is completely filled with boxes, tally up the initials.

3. Wild Checker Boards

Checkers are fun, but the boards are ho hum. With Kid Pix, you can make your own, and liven up the playing table. Create an eight squares by eight squares grid, and fill in alternating squares with the PAINT CAN. Then, use various WACKY BRUSH options to jazz up the board. You might break new ground in the field of checkerboard design!

Book Stuff

T his collection of activities involves making accessories for your child's library and a few for yours as well. The final products also make great gifts. Best of all, your child will enjoy being involved from design to printout.

1. Ex Libris

Bookplates are a time-honored way of identifying books from a personal library. Your child will probably enjoy using them all the more if he or she has a hand in creating them. A typical bookplate measures three inches by five inches and contains images as well as the name of the person who owns the book (you can always put the phrase "Ex Libris" or "From the Library of" to make the plate look official). Have your bookplate copied onto your child's favorite color paper, supply a glue stick, and your child is all set to personalize his or her library holdings. (You might even be able to convince your child to make some up for you, too.)

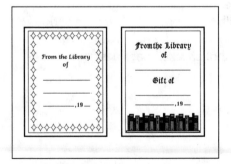

2. Bookmarks

Even the most riveting page-turner doesn't always get read in one sitting. Then you have a choice of dog-earing the page or finding a bookmark. Put your Kid Pix artist to work, and you'll have enough bookmarks to take care of all your reading needs. Your child can apply stamps, freeform drawings and doodles, or interesting swatches (great if you happen to have a color printer). You might want to draw a rectangular shape to confine your child's artistic efforts—the lines can be erased before printing. For lasting bookmarks, take your printouts to the local copy shop, and have them reproduced onto card stock. For added durability, consider laminating them. Then, settle into a good book, with the assurance that you'll never lose your place again.

3. Book Jacket Designers

As the old saying goes, you can't judge a book by its cover. But you certainly can spruce up a boring cover with a good Kid Pix design. Have your child create some "all purpose" covers that you can fold around paperbacks and small books, and put some spice in your reading life!

Flip Book

I n the age before pocket-sized action games, people sometimes used "flip books" to entertain themselves. Flip books are essentially an animation technique where an object is placed in a slightly different position on each page; so as the pages are rapidly flipped, the object appears to move smoothly. Here's how to create a flip book using Kid Pix. Your children just might flip for it.

1. Moving Stamp Images

Draw a rectangle on the screen that will print no bigger than two inches by three inches. Look through the stamps, and come up with an idea that you want to animate, such as an airplane taking off, a dog chasing a cat, a turtle crossing the road, the sun rising, and so on. Place your stamp in the desired position of the first screen, and add an appropriate background. Now, use the MAGNET option of the MOVING VAN to copy the whole picture (including the rectangle), and place it beside the first picture. Then, using the MOVING VAN tool, slightly shift the stamp to be animated. Keep repeating this until the stamp reaches the destination you had in mind.

Print out the rectangles (preferably on stiffer paper), then cut them out, without losing track of their order. Now, stack the rectangles so that the first picture is on the bottom of the pile. Staple the left side of the pages. Hold the left side and, with your thumb, flip the pages as you would a deck of cards. The stamp you've featured should be zooming across the pages!

2. Freeform Flip Book

If you feel limited by the stationary images of the stamps, create your own with the various drawing tools. For example, you can make "dancing" and "running" letters, a frowning face that changes to a smiling face, a winking eye, birds flapping their wings, or a swinging pendulum. Nothing is too zany for this fun little activity.

On Behalf of Our...

Everyone likes a pat on the back for doing a job well. And Kid Pix is a great way to create certificates of appreciation for all occasions. Here are some favorites in our household.

1. Anytime Certificate

You can make an all-purpose certificate of appreciation using many of the Kid Pix drawing tools. Start off with a border, perhaps by using the WACKY BRUSH and the GALAXY OF STARS option. You can also make a decorative border with repeating stamps. Then, select an appropriate typeface and style for the occasion. Save your file. Each time you create a new certificate, save it under a different name, so you preserve the master "template." OK, start the presses: A certificate a day keeps the blues away!

★★★★★★★★★★★★★★★★★★★★★★★★★★★★

In Appreciation of

_____

for

_____

_____

Official Family Member

★★★★★★★★★★★★★★★★★★★★★★★★★★★★

2. D.F.F., Dr. of Family Fun

Here's a certificate that you can present to someone who's made a good suggestion for a family outing, a read-aloud book, a trip to a museum, and so on. You might say something like, "Thanks for Your Great Idea to. . . ." (Leave space to hand write the suggestion.) Pick appropriate stamps to illustrate the idea, such as the picnic basket or bicycle.

3. Dust Busters

Who's made the biggest contribution to domestic affairs— er, housecleaning? Gin up a certificate for a family member who's recently helped put a room, drawer, or closet into ship-shape order (or kept one that way for more than a day). How about something like "In Recognition for a Generous Application of Elbow Grease"!

4. You Did It!

What a wonderful feeling to succeed at something after all that hard work! Draw and present a certificate to a family member who's achieved a sports, academic, or lifestyle modification goal, or finished a project. This could be the start of great things!

Kid Pix Calendars

Want something to look forward to each month? How about a snazzy new picture each month on your own personalized calendar? These activities suggest ways to use Kid Pix to create calendars that will be attractive additions to any wall or desk.

> *Note:* Each calendar consists of a picture (about two-thirds of the screen) and a simple calendar (on the bottom third). The numbers don't need to be boxed, merely aligned with the days of the week.

1. Person of the Month

Feature a family member each month, using the TEXT tool to note his or her most salient accomplishments—real or zany—such as the number of days on time for school, or the number of peas that the honoree ate in a week.

2. Backyard Scene of the Month

Have your child depict your backyard at different times of the year, noting seasonal changes. Perhaps a wading pool full of kids for August, a snowman and its creators for January, and a family of leaf-rakers and jumpers for October.

3. Neighborhood Scene of the Month

With this type of calendar, your child draws scenes of the community as it changes throughout the year. The pictures can show the park, neighboring families, school, and other important parts of your child's immediate world.

4. Animal of the Month

Have your child draw a picture of his or her favorite critters, much like nature calendars show different animals each month. The calendars can be serious, showing endangered species or zany, showing mythical beasts or imaginary creations from outer space.

5. Book of the Month

Here, your child illustrates a scene from favorite family books. Feature that book in your family dinner table discussions, puppet shows, and fantasy games. Perhaps look for other books by the same author as well.

6. Kid Pix Design of the Month

No criteria here, really. The calendar is simply whatever masterpiece your child and Kid Pix create.

Traditional Favorites

We all played with jigsaw puzzles and coloring books when we were kids. Now with Kid Pix, your children can get in on the act of designing and producing their own puzzles and pictures to color.

1. Jigsaws for Beginners

Have your child draw a picture, then use the PAINT CAN to fill the background with a solid color. Use the LINE tool with the thinnest point to divide the screen into nine squares. Print out the drawing, glue it to a piece of thin cardboard, allow it to dry, then cut out the pieces (your job). Voila! Instant puzzle.

2. Advanced Jigsaw Puzzle

Draw a pattern or screen collage, then use the WACKY PENCIL with the thinnest line to draw pieces. Draw a "bump" on every side, but alternate the direction so that there's a variety of shapes. Make the bumps large enough so they can be easily cut out. Print out the puzzle, and produce it as in the *Easy Jigsaw Puzzle*. (Note: Be sure to use very thin cardboard, such as the kind packaged with shirts, or else you may have difficulty cutting the pieces.)

3. The Ultimate Jigsaw Puzzle

Even the most challenging jigsaw puzzles have some clues on them, albeit small or repetitive ones. This one goes a step further. Just print out a solid sheet, cut it into puzzle pieces as in the preceding activity, and call it: "Meditation on Nothingness."

4. The Family Coloring Book

You can't buy a coloring book featuring your family, but your child can easily make one with Kid Pix. Have your child make simple line drawings of vacations and outings, family portraits, views of your house, favorite toys, and so on, without using solid colors as the fill. (Light screens can be used to highlight certain portions of the drawing.) Print out the pictures, and staple them together at the side. Your copy shop might also be able to make them into pads— they're great for the road or as gifts to younger siblings. Best of all, they'll have your child's personal touch.

Small Press

Here are some suggestions for booklets that your child can create and print out with Kid Pix. Perhaps this will be the beginning of a great career in the printing or publishing business!

Note: For all of the following booklets, suggest pages that are small enough to be folded and stapled in the middle. Alternatively, you can use full or half size pages, and staple the edges, or use a loose leaf notebook.

1. Cheer Me Up Books

What's the best way to get yourself out of a gloomy mood? A look at some inspirational drawings by your Kid Pix artist.

2. Blank Books

Yes, people actually buy blank books. Have your child create a dazzling cover, then staple it to some quality drawing or lined paper. Perfect for a personal diary.

3. Little Black Book

Everyone needs a good address book. Have your child create a page with repeating rules and spaces for names, addresses, and telephone numbers. You'll never be at a loss for key phone numbers again! (You might want to put the pages in a loose leaf notebook instead of stapling them.)

4. Personal Journal

A personal diary takes on new dimensions when you add drawings and pictures. Have your child print out records of daily feelings, last night's dreams, important events, and so on. Date them, and keep them in a special folder or notebook.

5. A Book of Books

How quickly we lose track of the books our kids read! Have your child create a booklet that lists and/or describes the books he or she has read—a true source of pride for your child. Make a list of books that your child would like to read in the future, too.

6. Family Records

Everybody can have his or her day in the sun with the Family Book of Records. The book (actually a notebook), contains sections for each person. Have your child use Kid Pix to jot down and perhaps illustrate his or her latest feat. "Completed Maze #9 in 23 seconds"!

Cutouts & Fold Outs

A ll you need to do these activities is a pair of safety scissors, tape or glue, some other common household items, and your Kid Pix printouts.

1. Kid Pix Puppeteers

Did you and your child do *Haute Couture* (page 54)? If so, here's a way to try out your spring fashions—on puppets. Create a set of people wearing your various designs, then print them out, and paste them to cardboard or laminate them with clear contact paper. Then, cut out the puppets (supervise carefully), and tape them to popsicle sticks, straws, or plastic knives (great way to recycle plastic ware). Your child can then put on the show of the year!

2. Designer Planes

Paper airplanes are all the more fun when they sport decorative wings and fuselages. Have your child create wild patterns, insignias, and so on, then print out the screen. Fold into paper airplanes, and watch the living room sky become a feast for the eyes.

3. Designer Vehicles

What will the car of the future look like? Have your Kid Pix engineer design one, and print it out. Paste the sheet to a piece of cardboard, or laminate it with clear contact paper. Then, tape on *L*-shaped pieces of cardboard so the vehicles stand up. Create a motor fleet, then sponsor a Kid Pix Grand Prix!

4. Designer Chains

Here's a way to breathe new life into an old activity—
making paper chains. Print out sheets of paper with
designs, lines of stamps, screens, and so on. Then, cut
them up into strips, and tape together loops for birthday
parties, Christmas tree decorations, bracelets, or just for
everyday fun.

5. Fancy Fans

Want to beat the heat from your monitor? Have your child
create a screenful of "cool" colors. Print out the screen,
then pass the paper through the printer again to print on
the back (assuming your printer can handle single sheets).
Fold the fan, then staple or paper clip the bottom. Now,
you and your child can keep cool while you do Kid Pix
activities.

Printed Matter

By this point, your child is probably an ace Kid Pix designer. Why not put those design skills to work, and create master art for all sorts of occasions? Take it to your local copy shop, and you'll have a great collection of useful and fun materials.

1. Make a Statement

Create personal stationery with flair—have your child use stamps or custom drawings to create personal or family logos (reproduce on quality paper stock).

2. Your Card, Please

No one's too young to hand out a business card. Have your child create snazzy-looking cards with a logo and job title, such as "Expert at Play," "Cookie Inspector," or "Full-time Kid." (Copy onto card stock.)

3. Doodle Dandy

Put the back sides of recycled paper to good use (unless you have tractor feed paper). Divide the screen into compartments, design a doodle-inspiring logo, print the page several times, then cut up your printouts into notepad-sized sheets. Happy doodling!

4. Someone Called You

Do phone messages sometimes slip through the cracks in

your house? Print up some phone message notes—same technique as that used for doodle sheets.

5. Remember This. . .

Do you have a memory like an elephant? If not, your Kid Pix designer can create some To-Do Lists with horizontal lines for all those tasks and errands. Print up enough to keep you on top of things—at least for this week!

6. Fine No More

Put an end to library fines! Have your child create a library books form with the due dates. With the pennies you save, you might be able to make significant additions to your own library.

7. The Family Nation

Every country has its own flag—why shouldn't your family? Have each person contribute an idea for a family flag. Post the printout by your doorway so all visitors can appreciate your sovereignty!

8. Door Knob Messages

Want to sleep in on the weekends? Have your child print out a "Sleep Zone" doorknob hanger, with a circle for the cutout. And for your child's room? Why of course, "Caution, Fun Inside. Kid Using Kid Pix"!

Appendix A

Kid Pix Crash Course: A Guide for the Impatient

A s we stressed earlier, you'll need some familiarity with Kid Pix before doing the activities in this book. If you're new to the program and insist on diving into the activities, scan through the following summary. You'll get a lot more out of the "crash course" if you experiment with the actual tools as you read about them. Follow the instructions supplied with your Kid Pix program to install and set up the software for your hardware.

Note: The PC version and the Mac version are slightly different, as will be indicated below. From here on, when we say "click," we mean press the single button on the Mac mouse, or the leftmost button on the PC mouse (you may have as many as three buttons).

Starting Kid Pix
Macintosh

Double click on Kid Pix program icon

IBM/Tandy/100% Compatibles: DOS

1. Change to the directory where you installed the Kid Pix program by typing

   CD\KIDPIX
   Press the Enter key

2. Type

KIDPIX

Press the Enter key

IBM/Tandy/100% Compatibles: Windows

Double click on the Kid Pix icon

Whether you're using a Macintosh or a PC (DOS or Windows), once you start Kid Pix, you'll see the program logo, a sign on-screen with whatever name you indicated when you installed the program, and finally the drawing screen shown in Figure 1, below.

The Lay of the Land

The drawing screen (Figure 1) is bordered on the top by the Menu Bar, to the left by the Tools, and on the bottom by various Tool Options.

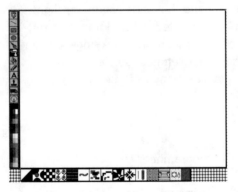

Figure 1. Kid Pix Drawing Screen

Menu Bar

The Menu Bar offers three "pull down" menus. Point to the option you wish to use, then click, and hold the mouse button. Drag the menu down to the option you wish to choose. Here's what each option does. (We've also listed the keyboard equivalents for the Mac and PC, which some people find faster than using the mouse. The Mac keyboard equivalents are listed by the Command key symbol ⌘ followed by a letter; PC keyboard shortcuts are listed by the Alt key plus a letter. When you use a keyboard equivalent, say "⌘ N" or "Alt+N," press the Command or Alt key, then without releasing it, also press the N key.)

File Menu

New   ⌘ N, Alt + N

Start a new file. Kid Pix clears the screen, first prompting you if you want to save anything that's already been drawn.

Open   ⌘ O, Alt + O

Retrieve a file that you've already created and saved.

Close   ⌘ W, (No PC shortcut)

Clear the screen that you're working on. Kid Pix will ask if you want to save anything that's on the screen.

Save   ⌘ S, Alt + S

Use this periodically to save a file as you work (always a good idea). When you enter the file name and select *OK*, Kid Pix will save your work to disk and continue. If the file already exists—you might be adding to one you've already created—Kid Pix will warn you, and ask if you want to overwrite it.

> *Note:* Even hard disks aren't foolproof. If you've been working for a long time on a drawing, don't wait until you're finished to save it. As a general rule, save your work *every* five minutes or so (gauge the interval by how much time you'd be willing to invest trying to recreate a picture in the event of a power glitch).

Save As **(No keyboard equivalents)**

Use this to save an existing file under a new name. Perhaps you've created a drawing, modified it, but don't want to lose it by overwriting it with the new version. Save the new drawing under a different name with *Save As*.

Page Setup **(No keyboard equivalents)**

This option sets up size, orientation, and other features of the page before you print.

Print ⌘ P, Alt + P

Use this menu option to print whatever you've drawn on the screen.

Quit ⌘ Q, Alt + Q

This exits the program, prompting you first to save whatever is on the screen.

Edit Menu

Undo ⌘ Z, Alt + U

This reverses your last action—and can be a lifesaver! You can also undo your last action by selecting the UNDO GUY from the tools column on the left. Select *Undo* (or the UNDO GUY) once to reverse an action, then select it again to "undo the undo."

Cut ⌘ X, Alt + X

This is used in conjunction with the MAGNET option (see ERASERS, below). When you select *Cut*, whatever you've highlighted is removed from the drawing screen, but stored in your computer's memory as long as you don't replace it with something else that you've cut, or turn off your system. You can later "paste" it onto another portion of the drawing screen.

Copy ⌘ C, Alt + C

Like *Cut*, this option stores in memory whatever object was highlighted by the MAGNET. Instead of removing the object from the drawing screen, however, it makes a clone wherever you select the *Paste* option. The highlighted object stays in memory until you replace it with something else or turn off your system.

Paste ⌘ V, ALT + V

If you've used *Cut* or *Copy*, this is how you'll move or clone the image to another portion of the screen. After moving the MAGNET to the "target area" and drawing a rectangle, you select the *Paste* option. Voila! Whatever you had cut or cloned appears in the rectangle.

Goodies Menu

Small Kids Mode On ⌘ K, Alt + K

This makes it easy for young children to use Kid Pix by turning off the Menu Bar, so the artists can't accidentally lose his or her work, or do something else undesirable. On the Mac, it also prevents the cursor from wandering off the drawing screen and into other programs. When you select Small Kids Mode, the words *Menu Bar* are replaced by *Kid Pix*. To restore the Menu Bar, click on *Kid Pix* and you will see a pull down option, *Show Menu Bar*. You can also restore the menu by pressing ⌘ M or Alt+M.

Edit Stamp ⌘ E, Alt + E

Stamps are pictures supplied with Kid Pix. Use this option to change the color of the stamp, modify the shape, rotate it, and make other alterations. You can even draw a totally new stamp of your own that will replace the Kid Pix stamp in the palette until you click on *Restore*, at which point the

original stamp will return to the palette. Refer to your
Broderbund manual for complete details.

Alphabet Text ⌘ A, Alt + A

This option allows you to enter letters that will "spill" out
of the WACKY BRUSH (see page 166). When you select it, a
window will open up with a space for you to write in the
pattern of letters that will flow from the brush. Enter up to
250 characters.

Tool Sounds ⌘ T, (No PC shortcut)

When you use the Kid Pix tools, you'll hear various sound
effects. If you don't want to hear them (perhaps you're
sneaking some computer time when everyone else is
asleep), use this option.

Record Sounds ⌘ R, (No PC shortcut)

With the Macintosh IIsi or LC, or an IBM PC equipped with
a sound board and running the Windows version of Kid
Pix, you can record sounds, and store them in your picture.
When you select the option, a dialog box opens up with
the options to *Record, Stop, Pause,* or *Play.* Use the options as you would any tape recorder. On a Mac, to hear
the recording without using the menu, simply press ⌘ H.
To halt the playback, press the Command ⌘ and Period
keys, or press the mouse button. The Option key speeds
up the playback, while the Spacebar slows it down. (With
a PC, you can only play back a recording through the
dialog box.)

Using the Tools and Options

The tools are located along the left side of the drawing
board. To select a tool, click on it, then move the cursor to
the drawing screen. The cursor will often change shape
when you get to the drawing screen, as described below.

Also, you can click on a color before choosing a tool; the tool will then use the selected color. At any time, you can move the cursor back to the color palette, and the tool will draw with the new color from that point on.

Each tool will be modified by various options that appear on the bottom of the screen in palettes. An arrow with a number at the right end of the option palette indicates that more options are available on additional palettes. Click on the arrow to change palettes.

Here is a brief description of the tools and their options. Try them as you read about each one. Also, refer to the Broderbund manual for details about each option.

Wacky Pencil

This tool allows you to draw lines of various thicknesses, textures, and colors (see Figure 2). When moved into the drawing screen, the cursor takes on the WACKY PENCIL shape. Press and hold the mouse button, then move the mouse. The pencil will draw a line until you release the button.

Two option palettes allow you to vary the thickness of the lines, to choose lines with rounded leading edges, and to draw with screens (dot patterns) of varying density. You can also create a "wash" effect. The QUESTION MARK option cycles through the colors of the rainbow as you move the pencil. (On monochrome systems, the QUESTION MARK cycles through various dot screens.)

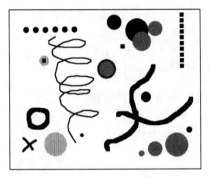

Figure 2. WACKY PENCIL *Tool*

Line ⟍

Like the WACKY PENCIL, the LINE tool allows you to make
lines of varying thicknesses, textures, and colors (see Figure
3). The difference is that these lines are always straight.
When you move the cursor into the drawing area, the
cursor will change to a crosshair. Press the mouse button to
"tack" the beginning of the line (at the crosshair position).
Continue holding the mouse button, then move the mouse
to the position where you want to end the line. When you
release the button, you will have a straight line.

The LINE option has one palette, and except for the WASH
and QUESTION MARK options, is identical to the first palette of
the WACKY PENCIL. (LINE has no "wash" feature, and the
QUESTION MARK creates a fan-like effect that inverts any
colors it sweeps over.)

To easily draw a vertical, horizontal, or 45-degree angle
diagonal line, begin drawing the line, then press the Shift
key. Release the mouse button before releasing the Shift
key, and you will have a perfect line.

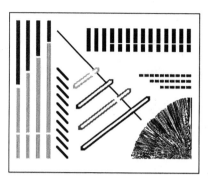

Figure 3. LINE *Tool*

Rectangle

This tool draws rectangles and squares that are clear, solid colored, or textured (see Figure 4). When you select the RECTANGLE and move the cursor to the screen, you will see a crosshair. Press and hold the mouse button, and "stretch" it to the diagonally opposite corner. Release the button, and a rectangular shape will appear on the screen. To draw a perfect square, press the Shift key as you draw the rectangle. Release the mouse button, then the Shift key, and the square will appear on the screen.

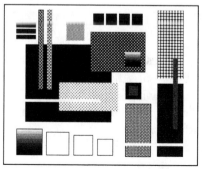

Figure 4. RECTANGLE *Tool*

A single option palette is available, and offers a variety of effects for creating transparent, solid, or patterned rectangles. The QUESTION MARK fills the rectangle with gradations of the rainbow or shades of gray (monochrome system). On a color system, you can also generate shades of gray by using the tool and holding the Option key (Mac) or Ctrl key (PC).

Oval

The OVAL tool is identical to the RECTANGLE, except that, as the name implies, it draws ovals and circles (see Figure 5). (For a perfect circle, use the Shift key in combination with the Oval tool.)

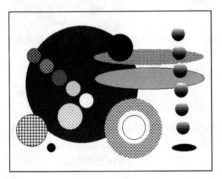

Figure 5. OVAL Tool

Wacky Brush

This tool leaves a swatch of interesting colored shapes or dot screens in its path (see Figure 6). After clicking on it and moving the cursor to the drawing screen, press and hold the mouse button to let the paint "flow." When you release the button, the brush stops painting.

Two option palettes offer effects such as spatter painting, tree silhouettes, branch shapes, pie shapes, geometric shapes, magnifying glass, zig zags, bubbles, dripping paint, "leaky pen," and lines of alphabet letters and other patterns. In addition, a built-in dot-to-dot tool creates an instant connect-the-dot drawing. Half of the options display additional effects if you press the Option key (Mac) or Ctrl key (PC) while using the WACKY BRUSH.

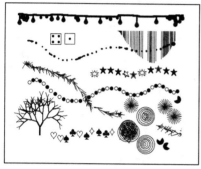

Figure 6. WACKY BRUSH Tool

Electric Mixer

This is the most unpredictable of the options and transforms your screen in various ways, depending on the options you select (see Figure 7).

The pallet of options allows you to change the whole screen image through inversions, adding random circles of color, checkerboards, raindrops, snowflakes, "broken glass," stripes, and other effects. It also can convert the screen into compartments with the same image in them.

Figure 7. ELECTRIC MIXER *Tool*

Paint Can

Use this tool to fill in any contiguous shapes on the drawing board, or the entire background. Note: "Contiguous" refers to line or color boundaries. The single option palette offers numerous textures in addition to solid fills. The QUESTION MARK fills in a rainbow of colors (or dot screens of black on a monochrome system).

Erasers

ERASER tools allow you to clean up the entire screen or specific objects. The options on the single palette include four erasers of different sizes for precision work and ten options for clearing the entire screen, such as the FIRECRACKER, which "explodes" after being moved to the screen (see Figure 8).

Figure 8. ERASER *Tool,* FIRECRACKER *Option*

Text A

When you select the TEXT tool, the alphabet letters and the numbers 0 through 9 appear as options on three palettes. Click on the TEXT icon, then click on the letter you wish to use. The cursor changes to that letter. Move the cursor to the drawing screen, and click the mouse button wherever you would like the letter to appear. If you hold the button and move the mouse, you'll create a stream of the letters. To enter text from the keyboard, press the Option key (Mac) or Ctrl Key (PC) while selecting the TEXT tool. This will display a new palette showing options for different typefaces and type sizes. Select an option and move the cursor to the drawing screen (it will have an *I*-beam shape). Click the mouse button, and text will appear on the screen as you type it from the position of the *I*-beam. It will also wrap at the end of the line like a regular word processor (see Figure 9). Move the cursor to another location and click to enter text elsewhere.

ABCDEFGHIJKLMNOPQRSTUVWXYZ
ABCDEFGHIJKLMNOPQRSTUVWXYZ 1234567890
𝔄𝔅𝔠𝔇𝔢𝔣𝔊𝔥𝔦𝔧𝔨𝔩𝔪𝔫𝔬𝔭𝔮𝔯𝔰𝔱𝔲𝔳𝔴𝔵𝔶𝔷 1234567890
ABCDEFGHIJKLMNOPQRSTUVWXYZ 1234567890
ABCDEFGHIJKLMNOPQRSTUVWX
ABCDEFGHIJKLMNOPQRSTUVWXYZ 1234567890
ABCDEFGHIJKLMNOPQRSTUVWXYZ 1234567890
ABCDEFGHIJKLMNOPQRSTUVWXYZ

Figure 9. TEXT *Tool*

Rubber Stamps

When you select the STAMP tool, you can choose from
among eight palettes worth of pictures, such as animals,
faces, vehicles, household objects, and so on (see Figure
10). Highlight the desired stamp, then move the cursor to
the drawing screen (the cursor becomes that stamp). When
you click the mouse button, the stamp picture will appear
on the screen. Hold the mouse button and move the
mouse to create a string of stamps.

Figure 10. RUBBER STAMP *Tool*

To double the size of a stamp, press and hold the Option key (Mac) or the Ctrl key (PC), then click the mouse. To triple the size, use the Shift key. For gargantuan stamps, use Option+Shift (Mac) or Ctrl+Shift (PC).

Moving Van

When you want to move portions of the screen from one position to another, use the MOVING VAN tool. When you select MOVING VAN, a blinking dashed box appears on the screen. Move the box to the objects to be moved, and press and hold the mouse button. Then, drag the object to the desired position. Release the mouse button, and the object will stay in its new position. The options provide different size and shape MOVING VAN boxes for precision screen rearrangements.

To copy an object, press and hold the Option key (Mac) or Ctrl key (PC) during the whole moving operation. When you release the mouse button, a duplicate of the object will appear in the new position.

To make a custom MOVING VAN box, use the MAGNET option. A crosshair appears on the screen. Draw a rectangle around the object. The crosshair then changes to a magnet. Move the magnet inside the rectangle, then drag the rectangle by holding the mouse button and releasing it at the desired location. Note that the other MOVING VAN boxes don't move solid white backgrounds; the MAGNET does. Finally, in lieu of the Option (Mac) and Ctrl (PC) keys, you can use the MAGNET with the *Copy*, *Cut*, and *Paste* commands from the *Edit* menu located on the Menu Bar above the drawing screen.

Undo

See above, *Undo* option, *Edit* menu.

Appendix B

Kid Pix Problem-Solver: Troubleshooting

Kid Pix is an extremely "well-behaved" program. Still, all software can run into problems, and most Kid Pix problems will be one of the following:

MACINTOSH

1. **Problem**: You get an error message that you don't have enough memory.

   Solution: Click *once* on the program icon, then choose *Get Info*. If you're using a pre-System 7.1 operating system, the lower right hand corner of the information box will display two numbers for memory: *Suggested* and *Current*. Make sure that the *Current* is at least the same or greater than the *Suggested*. If you still get the error message, change the *Current* to one-and-a-half times the *suggested* (assuming that you have enough memory in your computer).

   If you have System 7.1 installed on your computer, then you will see three numbers in the information box: *Suggested*, *Minimum*, and *Preferred*. Make sure that the *Minimum* and *Suggested* number are the same, and that the *Preferred* number is one-and-a-half times the *Minimum*.

1. **Problem**: No sound, or not the full range of sounds (including vocalizations of alphabet letters and numbers).

   Solution: Make sure that all of the Kid Pix files are in the same folder. As a general rule, don't mess with Kid Pix once you've installed it; everything is where it's supposed to be.

3. **Problem**: No stamp palettes.

   Solution: Same cause as the sound problem. Same solution, too.

4. **Problem**: Application unexpectedly quits, or the system "locks up" (it doesn't respond to the keyboard, and you have to power it off).

   Solution: Select the *Control Panels* from the Apple in the upper left hand corner of the Menu Bar for your desktop. Then select the *Memory* icon. You'll see options for *Virtual Memory* and *32-Bit Address*. Turn them both off, close the control panel, then restart your computer.

   If you're still having problems, try holding down the Shift key when you restart your computer. This will disable any extensions that may be affecting Kid Pix.

IBM PC/COMPATIBLES DOS/WINDOWS

1. **Problem**: You can't create an owner's name file.

   Solution: Your CONFIG.SYS file doesn't contain enough files or buffers. The file must contain a line that reads *FILES=25* and *BUFFERS=25*. If you don't know how to edit your CONFIG.SYS file, contact someone who can help you. Once the file has been changed, you must reboot your computer for the changes to take effect.

2. **Problem**: The system locks up after certain sounds are made.

   Solution: Check your sound board installation. Sound boards can cause a variety of quirky problems that manifest themselves irregularly. If you don't know you way around "interrupts," "DMA Channels," and the like, get help from someone who does. The good news is that once you get a sound board properly configured, you should have trouble-free computing.

3. **Problem**: No sounds; system locks up.

   Solution: While a sound board may be the culprit, you might also have a memory problem. Kid Pix needs 540K of *free* memory. So if you have TSR's (pop-up programs that work within other programs), try turning them off to free up the memory you need.

   Also, if you are using Stacker, you cannot operate Kid Pix unless you create an "unstacked" partition on your hard disk, then reinstall Kid Pix in the uncompressed area. Consult your Stacker manual for details.

4. **Problem**: You can't use your mouse.

   Solution: Make sure you have the most current version of your mouse driver. This generally solves the problem.

Index

Index Categories

A = Artistic and drawing skill builders
E = Electronic versions of traditional games
G = Group and party activities
L = Language, communication, & reading skill builders
M = Math skill builders
O = Suited for older kids
P = Powers of observation/memory/mind
Q = Quick studies (low preparation time)
Y = Suited for younger kids

About the Authors

S teve and Ruth Bennett are nationally-recognized leaders in developing activities for quality family time. Their *365 TV-Free Activities You Can Do With Your Child* (Bob Adams, Inc.) is one of the nation's best selling parenting books, and now has more than 200,000 copies in print. It has been cited in *USA Today*, the *Wall Street Journal*, *Parent's Magazine*, *McCall's* (named Best TV-Free Alternative for 1992), and many national and regional newspapers and magazines. Steve and Ruth have discussed parenting issues on more than 250 radio talk shows. Their other parenting titles include: *Kids' Answers to Life's Big Questions* (Bob Adams, Inc.), *365 Outdoor Activities You Can Do with Your Child* (Bob Adams, Inc.), and two additional titles in the Random House/Broderbund Family Computing Series—*The Official Playroom Activity Book*, and *The Official Treehouse Activity Book*.

Steve Bennett is full-time author who has written more than forty books on subjects ranging from business management and computing to environment and parenting. He holds a master's degree in Regional Studies from Harvard University, where he studied Chinese geomancy, the ancient art of siting tombs and houses.

Ruth Loetterle Bennett is a landscape architect, author, and illustrator. She holds an M.L.A. from the University of Virginia, and has designed playgrounds and public parks throughout the country.

Steve and Ruth live with their children, Noah 6 and Audrey 3, in Cambridge, Massachusetts.

CONTEST RULES

Note: By submitting materials to this contest, all entrants acknowledge that the materials are the sole property of Steve and Ruth Bennett and will not be returned. As a condition of contest participation, each entrant agrees that if his or her entry is selected as a winner, then the entrant (and parent or guardian if the entrant is under 18 years of age) will sign an affidavit of eligibility and a formal release permitting publication of the ideas and materials submitted and assign all proprietary rights therein to Steve and Ruth Bennett. Failure to comply will result in an alternate winner being selected. Void where prohibited law. No purchase necessary. One entry per person. Broderbund and Random House employees and their families are not eligible.